JUST ITALIAN

ITALIA

A Guide to Italian Restaurants
In and Around Seattle

Just Italian

Merilee Frets

JOHNSTON
ASSOCIATES
INTERNATIONAL

P.O. BOX 313
MEDINA, WASHINGTON 98039

ISBN: 1-881409-01-5

The listings and information appearing in this edition were
current at the time of the final editing, but are subject to
change at any time. No gratuities of any kind have been
solicited or accepted from listed firms.

First printing October, 1992
Cover art and book design by Mike Jaynes
Production by Kate Perrett

JASI
Post Office Box 313
Medina, Washington 98039 U.S.A.
(206) 454-7333

Printed in the United States of America
Distributed in Canada by Raincoast Books Ltd.

TABLE OF CONTENTS

Acknowledgments

Thank you to the following people and organizations who were instrumental in the preparation of this book:

Tom Frets at G. Raden & Sons Distributors,

Carrie Omegna at deGustibus Wine Imports,

and John Bonnier, whose genius with food, good humor and natural teaching abilities are a continuing inspiration to me.

PREFACE

Just Italian! is intended to be a guide to the rich variety of Italian restaurant styles we are fortunate to have in our midst. It does not attempt to rate the restaurants (i.e., "outstanding," "good," "acceptable"), which is more appropriately done when the response to a review can be immediate. Nor do we include every single Italian restaurant in the area.

You wouldn't seek the same kind of restaurant after a softball game as you would with an important business client or favorite dinner companion. Thus what you find here is information to help you make your dining choice: descriptions of ambiance (casual or upscale, authentic or "Italian-inspired"), size, accepted methods of payment, representative prices, descriptions of menu items (imaginative, authentic or predictably traditional), ease of parking, mention of good wine lists, whether or not there is live entertainment and other significant information that distinguishes the particular restaurant. Certainly if the food was good when I ate there, I say so!

Children are welcomed at every restaurant. However, menu offerings, prices and seating arrangements are more accommodating to children at some places than at others. In addition to the notation at the bottom of each restaurant review, the Index at the back of the book includes a convenient compilation of those places most appropriate for children.

Finally, restaurants are a quicksilver business. Some may not be where they were when I visited them; conversely, others may have opened since we went to press. Over this we have no control, so I invite you to write me and share your own discoveries and observations for inclusion in a subsequent edition of *Just Italian!*

c/o JASI
P.O. Box 313
Medina, WA 98039

INTRODUCTION

In recent years, Americans in general and Seattleites specifically have gone crazy over Italian food. It seems that when a neighborhood sprouts a new restaurant, it's very often Italian. The supermarket freezer case is loaded with microwaveable lasagne, pizza, and stuffed manicotti. Major beverage companies now own strings of pizza parlors, and big-city chefs have become overnight sensations creating and selling "designer-original" pizzas. Pasta has become familiar to us relatively recently as "pasta". It used to be called "noodles" or "macaroni". Remember?

Because you're interested enough in Italian food to buy this book, you've likely done your part to popularize the trend. But I must tell you that something happened to *real* Italian food as it made its way into popular acceptance on American tables. I call it "the American Intrusion," and it expresses itself something like this: overcooked pasta smothered by a load of garlic-laden tomato or heavy cream sauce; white bread that tastes like paper slathered with garlic butter; meatballs—indeed, too much meat—served as a main entree with pasta and plenty of melted cheese oozing in and around that overcooked pasta. While

Italians love their pungent cheeses and eat plenty of garlic and pasta, I am describing what *we Americans* have come to think of as Italian food.

Perhaps a little history and a brief discussion of the characteristics of good Italian food will add to your appreciation of this incredible cuisine. The more discriminating you become in your dining choices, the more you will appreciate the really good bistros and trattorias here in Seattle.

The majority of Italian immigrants came to the United States during the late 1800's and early 1900's, bringing with them perhaps the richest culinary heritage in the world. Italy is bordered on three sides by the sea and to the north by the Alps shared with France, Austria and Switzerland. Its interior, too, is divided by numerous mountain ranges. For centuries, it functioned as a collection of some 20 regions, each one with its own name and strong identity: Tuscany, Veneto, Emilia-Romagna, Lombardy, Umbria, Campania, Calabria to name a few. These natural boundaries kept travel, trade and foreign influence among regions to a minimum; thus each region developed its own style, customs and temperament, as well as recipes served only on for its own tables.

As in art and literature, culinary genius is often an expression of a culture's richness. The Renaissance was born in Florence, and its creators certainly did not leave their aesthetic sensibilities behind when they stepped into the kitchen. In fact, the Italians taught the French to cook. Italian cuisine was so highly evolved when Catherine de Medici married Henry II of France in the mid-sixteenth century that she was compelled to bring an entourage of Italian chefs from Florence with her to teach the French court chefs how to cook properly. Table etiquette in France moved up a notch, too, as Italians introduced the use of forks. Classical French cuisine, used as the benchmark the world over for originality and method, actually has its roots in classical Italian style.

Florence is in Tuscany, which is among the northern regions of Italy that include Emilia-Romagna, Piedmont, Lombardy, Liguria, Veneto and others. Today communication and transportation systems have reduced the historic geographic barriers among the 20 regions of Italy, but the cuisine of northern Italy still bears its legendary dominance with an emphasis on fresh vegetables, risotto, polenta, pasta, light pungent cheeses, legumes, mushrooms and soups. Beef, pork and fish are favorite meats. Grilling of meats and vegetables is highly popular. Flavoring everything are fresh herbs such as sweet basil, sage, bay leaves, thyme, capers and rosemary. Olive oil or butter are the essential cooking fats, depending on the region. Homemade pastas are the flavor carriers for red and cream sauces. Wine is made by virtually anyone with enough ground to grow some vines, and no meal is complete without wine. Crusty, coarsely-textured bread is as important to the meal as the wine. Onions and garlic are, of course, used; but flavors are balanced, not dominant. This is a very healthy way to eat!

Southern regions include Campana, Calabria, Latium (Rome), Abruzzi, Apulia and Sicily. It's this style of Italian food that prevails in America, simply because most of the people who came here from Italy are from the warmer regions south of Rome. Meals from these regions emphasize foods that come from seaside villages in an intense climate: fresh fish, hearty nose-filling cheeses, fresh vegetables, fresh-made gnocchi and pastas, rich (sometimes fiery) tomato sauces and garlic. Southern Italians cook with cured olives and anchovies to add the saltiness and pungency that is characteristic of their food. Olive oil is the essential cooking fat. The fragrance of herbs like oregano, sage, mint, basil, rosemary, parsley and thyme pervade every dish. Bread and wine are equally important in the meal. This, too, is a very healthy way to eat!

Food is a connecting ritual with Italian families and friends. That is why food and cooking play such an important part in the Italian way of living. Italian cooking consistently embodies three basic elements: instinct, the whim of the cook, and whatever ingredients are on hand. These are combined to create something to share with people you love.

Simplicity and freshness are woven into every recipe. Meals are multi-course events whose ingredients may vary according to the season and, again, the whim of the cook. Fresh vegetables are every bit as important as pasta, and the vegetables that are in season are best of all. In fact, the role of vegetables often define the meal.

By way of illustration, let's look at the main courses you'll find most often on menus of Italian restaurants. Contrary to popular interpretation here in the U.S., Italian courses are small. An *antipasto* may be only anchovies served with butter and crusty bread, or a few slices of wonderful salami, prosciutto and melon. In a restaurant, they are traditionally conspicuously displayed to whet your appetite. We Americans have come to expect an antipasti platter rather than a small portion of simple fare. (a result, perhaps, of our "more must be better" attitude.)

The first course (*primi*) is always a pasta, risotto or soup. The incomparable variety of Italian soups is magnificent: beans and pasta, rice and celery, potato and onion, split pea and potato, lentil and many made with shellfish. With such a rich tradition of soups available, it mystifies me that American Italian restaurants confine themselves primarily to minestrone (vegetable) soup. Since most of the soups are northern Italian-inspired, and most of our restaurants are southern-Italian owned, this may be the logical explanation.

It's my opinion that we least understand the amazing number and seemingly infinite variety of pastas with their combinations of sauces, vegetables and cheeses. Perfectly cooked pasta has an *al dente* texture: that is, it gives some resistance in the chewing process. In good homemade pasta that is fresh and expertly cooked, you can still taste the earthy edges of the flour.

Whether it is stuffed with vegetables or an Italian cheese, or laced with an aggressive puttanesca sauce, the pasta should act as a "flavor *carrier*." It shouldn't be loaded with sauce or laden with cheese; rather, it should carry the multiple flavors of those ingredients to your palate. A good pasta experience is simple and sensual! Oh, one more word about pasta: rarely in Italy is pasta eaten in combination with meat. Shellfish, anchovies, eggplant, and perhaps a good pancetta (bacon) or Bolognese sauce, yes.

But not meatballs, which are an American intrusion born out of our 1950's need for meat and starch together.

Risottos (rice-based dishes) are divine if the rice has been cooked properly. In restaurants that is oftentimes a tricky business. Like pasta, rice is combined with an endless variety of ingredients (remember "what's on hand and the whim of the cook"), and it, too, acts as a flavor carrier. For lack of a better description, I'll characterize risotto as an Italian pilaf, because the cooking method involves sauteeing rice in butter and onions and simmering it in a flavored stock. You can imagine just how delicious risotto might be with vegetables or cheeses, or a pungent tomato sauce and shellfish.

Other first course dishes are made with *gnocchi* and *polenta*. In Seattle, we're just starting to catch on to these two extremely popular Italian foods. Gnocchi are small and dumpling-like and are made with pureed potato or semolina. They may be stuffed with any number of combinations of things—ground veal, cheese, pureed vegetables, for example—then boiled in water like pasta and served with pesto or a tomato or cream sauce. If you see gnocchi on the menu, order it and become familiar with the different ways local Italian cooks make it. A number of places in Seattle claim they make the best gnocchi in the city. You be the judge of that!

Popular in northern Italian regions, polenta is a dense, robust version of American cornbread. Cornmeal is cooked with water, then allowed to set up so it can be sliced into squares. (Of course, onions, peppers, or other flavors may be added.) After the polenta sets, cooks do any number of things with it. It is wonderful grilled together with fresh vegetables, or topped with a pungent tomato sauce and a sausage, or even served alone broiled hot with cheese. I prefer a coarse-grained polenta because it's closer to what is found in northern Italy. You'll discover that only a few places in town make it that way.

The second course (*secondi*) is often shown on Italian restaurant menus as "*Pesce e Carne*" (fish and meat), or "*Pollo*" (chicken), or "*Vitello*" (veal)—or any number of other ways.

This is the meat course; and generally it is kept quite simple. Eggs are often used, too. (Where do you think those wonderful frittatas originated?) In the United States, we place great emphasis on meat and it's widely available. In the early years of Italian restaurant development, proprietors sought to please the public and did as Americans did: they served meat and starch together. Like the other courses, meats are prepared any number of imaginative ways to include sauces, vegetables and cheeses.

In really fine restaurants, a salad (*insalate*) follows the second course. But that's not what we're accustomed to here, so Italian restaurants have accomodated our preferences.

With respect to Italian desserts (*dolci*), they have more prominence on menus in America than in Old Country kitchens. How anyone can eat dessert after an antipasto, a sumptuous pasta or risotto, a salad, and/or a lightly-sauced fish or other meat and vegetables is absolutely beyond me, especially at 8 o'clock at night! Besides, most of the desserts you find on your local Italian menus have been prepared elsewhere by professional dessert-makers. If there's a "*dolci del giorno*" (dessert of the day), it may have been made by the cook or someone else in the restaurant. Ask your server. There are, however, several exceptions that I encourage you to order because they are so Italian and so rarely found here. One is zabaglione, an incredible whipped egg/marsala mixture that is spooned over fresh fruit or eaten alone or in cream puffs. Another is carmello, a custard-like dessert served with whipped cream and perhaps slivered almonds or pecans. I realize that tiramisu and infinite varieties of cheesecakes have become very trendy and are subject to endless debate; but for my tastes, a little fruit is the best finish to an Italian repast.

In summary. . .in your quest for your favorite little trattoria, please remember that a good one extends its table to you. They want to make you happy and feed you well. You'll know that by the originality and freshness of the specials and the menu items and the comfort you feel just being there. I have a positive bias for those that change menus and specials according to the season and who take pains to offer excellent wine and bread. Without question, we have some fine places here in Seattle, ones that embody the elegant simplicity and zest for life which are the grand heritage of Italian cuisine. It is my hope that you will use this guidebook to become a more discriminating patron of your favorite places and to discover new delights.

Merilee Frets

AL BOCCALINO

Location:	1 Yesler Avenue, Seattle
Phone:	622-7688
Days/Hours:	Lunch: Tues-Fri 11:30-2
	Dinner: Mon-Sat 5:30-10
Reservations:	Recommended on weekends

An understated half-round green awning covers the door of Al Boccalino at the west end of Yesler Avenue. This restaurant sings of New York. Not too stylish, not too uptown, but definitely that left-of-center, Mario Cuomo feel. Al Boccalino is on my "must go" list for friends and visitors.

The arched windows and exposed brick walls lend a rustic, almost cozy, feel to the interior. But this is not your "cozy little trattoria". It's a polished, exciting place; a place to be and be seen—casual á la Ralph Lauren. And the food is good, very good.

In owner Kenny Raider's words, "A menu is a menu. A recipe is a recipe. It's the execution that gives the food life." Diners can expect spontaneous excitement from Raider and his chef Tim Roth. From the specials, my companion and I chose an antipasto of grilled polenta with local porcini mushrooms, marsala wine and mascarpone cheese for $7.50. As an entrée, we chose a risotto alla pescatora (rice with sea scallops, prawns, calamari) for $12 and a fettuccine with prawns, roasted red and yellow peppers, toasted pine nuts, and swiss chard for $13.50. Neither of us left a bite on our plates. Entrée prices range from $11.50-$19. Salads, antipasti, and desserts are á la carte.

The wine cellar is small but selective, and includes some superb Italian reds and whites priced from $18-$35.

47 Seats • Beer and wine • Tight wheelchair access, none to restrooms • Free metered parking after 6 pm, also paid private lots • Small waiting area Smoking in designated area • *Credit cards:* **VISA M/C Local checks**

ANGELINA'S

Location:	2311 California, Seattle
Phone:	932-7311
Days/Hours:	Breakfast: Mon-Fri 6:30-11, Sat-Sun 8-3
	Lunch: Daily 11-5
	Dinner: Mon-Thurs 5-11, Fri-Sun 5-12
Reservations:	Recommended for weekend dinner

Angelina's is the perfect definition of a neighborhood restaurant. I felt as if I had wandered into a Grange hall from the Fifties. High ceiling fans, shelves of empty wine bottles ringing the walls and swinging screen doors amplify the comfortable expansiveness inside. There's a piano in the main dining room, which adds to the feeling that this is the kind of place where the mood of the moment might inspire someone to spring up and play "As Time Goes By."

On Spaghetti Mondays, your second helpings of spaghetti with meat sauce or marinara are free. "Fun With Pasta" kids' menus with dot-to-dot and color-me pictures teach kids that "Italians eat their spaghetti and fettuccine by twirling it around their forks. Can you?" Clearly this is an ideal restaurant for families, a dinner for two, or a gathering of friends and neighbors.

The daily menu includes pasta ($5.35-$8.50), antipasti ($3.25-$6.50), soups and salads ($5-$6), and chicken, veal and oven-baked entrees ($8-$12.50). Caffe Mauro and choices of good Italian wines accompany your meal. Chef Jim Ridley enhances the menu with daily specials. As with the other Mitchelli Family Restaurants, the style of the food here is "fused"; that is, it is not dominated by a clearly southern or northern influence.

99 Seats • Beer and wine • Easy wheelchair access Free on-street parking • Smoking permitted in designated area • Children welcome • *Credit cards:* VISA M/C Discover AmEx Local checks

ANTIPASTI

Location:	83 King Street, Seattle
Phone:	622-6743
Days/Hours:	Lunch: Mon-Sat 11:30-3
	Dinner: Mon-Thurs 5-10:30,
	Fri-Sat 5-11:30, Sun 5-9
Reservations:	Advised, especially for lunch

At last! A stylish Italian "grazing" bar for the hip and the hungry. Carmine Smeraldo, who also owns Il Terrazzo, has operated a succession of restaurants in this same location. The current concept is great! The menu (wear your glasses, it's set in teensie-weensie type) includes 13 antipasti choices, soups and salads, pizza and calzone, 13 pasta dishes and a half-dozen entree selections with fish, chicken, lamb and beef.

Antipasti's serves portions versus single-plate meals. The pasta dishes may be ordered in an antipasti size *or* a platter size that is more than enough for two persons. The Pizza Arlecchino can be purchased by the foot or the yard ($29). Antipasti selections are original and unlike anywhere else in the city: Radicchio Caprino (grilled radicchio filled with goat cheese and pine nuts for $4.75) and Melanzane Aglio e Olio (Italian eggplant baked with parmesan and mozzarella for $3.95) are noteworthy. Add a salad, and you have a complete meal.

Platter sizes for pasta dishes range $11.95-$15.95; single portions are $5.25-$6.50. Entrées run $8.50-$12.95. Pizzas and calzones come in nine-inch rounds and are $6.95-$8.95. Given the friendly prices, the stylish surroundings and the good service, Antipasti is perfect as a place to unwind after work or for gathering before or after Kingdome events.

248 Seats • Full bar • Wheelchair access • Parking in paid lots and metered on-street • Waiting area Smoking in designated area • *Credit cards:* VISA M/C AmEx Disc Diners Local checks

ARMONDO'S CAFE ITALIANO

Location:	919 S. 3rd, Renton
Phone:	228-0759
Days/Hours:	Lunch: Mon-Fri 11-4
	Dinner: Mon-Wed 4-9, Thurs-Sun 4-10
Reservations:	Not accepted. Call ahead to see how busy they are.

It's been said that there are two reasons to go to Renton: one is Boeing, the other is Armondo's in the old downtown area.

Opened in May 1986 by George Armondo Pavone (Renton High, Class of '80; mom works at Boeing, dad is a Renton police officer), this restaurant springs from deep roots in the city. Pavone's timing couldn't have been better when he opened the little "pizza by the slice" joint downtown. The demand for Italian food was on the rise, and his little outlet was the only game in town. Now a full-service family restaurant that seats 80 people, Armondo's serves Italian-inspired food, and plenty of pizza, to legions of loyal customers willing to wait patiently for a table.

Armondo's sticks with patrons' preferences and does not vary the menu greatly. Fettuccini is the house specialty. Dishes combined with chicken, smoked salmon (they smoke their own) and Alfredo sauce are customers' top choices. The influence is southern Italian, with plenty of sauces and cheeses topping the entrees. The calzone and pizzas are baked in a wood-burning brick oven. Wines are a mix of Italian and domestic. Lunch prices are $4.95-$6.95, and dinners are priced $5.95-$11.95. All menu items are available for take-out.

80 Seats • Beer and wine • Wheelchair access
Free on-street parking • No waiting area
Children welcome • Smoking in designated area
Credit cards: VISA M/C AmEx Local checks

AVÉ! RISTORANTE

Location:	4743 University Way NE, Seattle
Phone:	527-9830
Days/Hours:	Lunch: Mon-Fri 11:30-2:30
	Dinner: Sun-Thurs 5-10, Fri-Sat 5-11
Reservations:	Not necessary

Located on "The Ave" in the heart of the U-District, Avé! is a great place to grab a good, predictable Italian lunch or dinner for a decent price. Owners Gianfranco and Juli D'Aniello opened Avé! in 1985 and have created a cheerful trattoria that puts you at your ease and welcomes kids (they even eat free on Sundays from the special children's menu). The dark green ceiling and soft lighting contrast with the brightly covered tables, and you can hear the friendly clattering of pans in the kitchen while your meal is being prepared — certainly more of a comfort than a distraction.

Gianfranco does most of the cooking. He serves up 10 kinds of pizza priced $6-$7.50, and calzone. The menu includes the usual pasta dishes like spaghetti alle vongole and penne puttanesca, as well as entrees with chicken, veal and seafood. The two specials the night we stopped in were "Gnocchi Vesuvio" with tomato sauce and fresh basil and a delicious grilled swordfish, which was cooked to perfection. Entree prices range $7.50-$12.95. Good selections of wine by the glass run $3.50-$5.

The lunch menu is a slightly modified version of the dinner menu and emphasizes pizzas, salads and pasta. Prices range $5-$8.

60 Seats • **Beer and wine** • **Wheelchair access**
On-street metered parking • **Small entry/waiting
area** • **Smoking in designated area** • **Children
welcome** • *Credit cards:* **VISA M/C AmEx DISC
Local checks**

BARLEE'S FAMILY PIZZA and PASTA

Location:	3410 Fremont Ave., Seattle
Phone:	633-4545
Days/Hours:	Mon-Thurs 11-10, Fri-Sat 11-11,
	Sat-Sun 11:30-11
	Lunch and dinner: same menu
Reservations:	Not necessary

We all have our local faves, and this is one of mine for sentimental reasons. In 1989 Barlee's was called something else, and it was pretty much a dive. But we liked the Italian-style salad, the bread with whipped garlic butter, the house Chianti, and the floor-to-ceiling windows that permit full view of the funky Fremont scene, so we kept coming back.

After managing the restaurant for three years, Lee and Barbara Agelopoulos bought it in 1991, renamed it, and remodeled. They re-upholstered the booth seats, added new tables and chairs and painted the walls (like I said, this place was kind of a dive). It hasn't lost any of its neighborhood charm or loyal customers, and the service is still friendly. Patrons come with family and friends, or alone with a book to just hang out.

Lee is Greek, but his offerings are primarily Italian: shrimp Milano, standard pasta dishes made with manicotti, rigatoni and spaghetti, and a number of very good pizzas (we especially like the vegetarian). Daily specials cooked by Lee round out the menu. Prices range from $3.55-$8.95, and pizzas are $3.15 for an individual size and up to $15.95 for the Barlee's Special.

**90 Seats • Beer and Wine • Easy wheelchair access
Ample free parking (note: busy streets in Fremont)
Smoking permitted in designated area • Children
welcome • *Credit cards:* VISA M/C Local checks**

BELLA LUNA

Location:	143rd & Greenwood Avenue N., Seattle
Phone:	367-5862
Days/Hours:	Brunch: Sat-Sun 8-3
	Lunch: Mon-Fri 11-4, Sat-Sun 3-5
	Dinner: Sun-Thurs 5-10, Fri-Sat 5-11
Reservations:	Recommended for dinner

Everywhere you look there are moons on the walls...moons rising over the Space Needle, photos of the HoneyMOONers, moon-shaped mirrors, and even a poster of Moonstruck Cher. Such is the whimsey throughout Bella Luna. ("There's a moon out in our neighborhood every night of the week.")

Bella Luna shares the same menu and owners with Stella's, Trattoria Mitchelli and Angelina's, but it has added pizzas and calzones to the offerings. Weekend brunch here is a popular occasion and deserves mention. American breakfast items are served with an Italian accent: Italian sausages, roma tomatoes, romano cheese, artichokes, eggs di Palermo — and who could forget Italian Toast, which is "justa like Frencha Toasta only better." This is a wonderful place for family and friends to enjoy the food and congeniality of a neighborhood restaurant.

Though the restaurant sits on the busy north end of Greenwood Avenue, wooden fencing and blooming foliage screen off the traffic and activity. Diners can focus on their companions (how romantic!) or put the daily grind aside for a while. We happened to stop by in the afternoon for a rich cup of Caffe Mauro and a sinful Crema in Tazzine. Other customers were sipping wine and catching up on the Days of Their Lives.

120 Seats • Full bar • Tight wheelchair access
Free parking in adjacent lot • No waiting area
Smoking permitted in designated area • Children
welcome • *Credit cards:* **VISA M/C AmEx Local**
checks

BIZZARO ITALIAN CAFE

Location:	1307 North 46th, Seattle
Phone:	545-7327
Days/Hours:	Dinner: Mon-Sun 4:30-10
Reservations:	Not accepted

Bizzaro founder and owner David Nast claims he named his cafe for one he visited in London years ago. I prefer to think the name is a metaphor for the ambiance. Huge cut-out celestial bodies hang from the ceiling (David tells me he changes his ceiling regularly; a magic carpet ride is next). Masks suggesting wanton culinary rites stare expectantly from the walls. Instead of the Italian tenor singing on tape, it's k.d.lang and Bob Dylan. The building was once an auto body shop, converted to an aerobics studio, converted to a yoga studio, converted to a cafe. I hope it stays a cafe because I love this place. I keep expecting Tom Robbins or Gary Larsen to wander in.

David's Wallingford location is perfect for showcasing his talent for food and his zest for the experimental. Appetizers, salads, and a "Mix and Match" section of pastas with sauces, plus customers' enduring favorites (labelled "Bizzaro's Tried and True") spring from a fusion of northern and southern Italian cuisine. Generally there are three nightly specials. A house specialty is chicken and artichoke hearts in a light homemade pesto. Be sure to order an antipasto plate of bread served with a ramekin of roasted garlic puree — all those little taste buds on the back of your tongue will shout "wahoo."

Dinner prices are $6.95-$10.95. The wine list is modestly priced and eclectic.

50 Seats • Beer and wine • Wheelchair access Free parking on surrounding streets • No waiting area • No smoking • *Credit cards:* VISA M/C DISC Local checks

BOTICELLI

Location:	303 Occidental, Seattle
Phone:	343-0501
Days/Hours:	Mon-Sat 11-12
	Lunch and dinner: same menu
Reservations:	Accepted but not required

Owner Angelo Belgrano is from the coastal town of Savona in northern Liguria. He is determined to keep Boticelli's food as simple and elegant as that from his native region. The recipes are mostly Angelo's, plus additions from his manager, Paolo Domeneghetti. Their specialty is gnocchi served with a variety of accompaniments that include tangy wild game sauce, four cheeses, a bell pepper cream sauce and a tomato sauce. Antipasti, grilled Italian sandwiches, and a simple roast pork, lamb or chicken come from the grill daily and are accompanied by fresh vegetables.

The restaurant is a stylish interpretation of an Italian trattoria with outdoor seating in the Occidental Street Plaza at Pioneer Square. When I was there (and I believe to Boticelli's credit), three tourists from Ohio walked in wanting spaghetti and meat balls and refused the server's suggestion of "the best gnocchi in the city." They fled elsewhere — and the ad-agency types from adjacent businesses smiled smugly and continued savoring their polenta and char-grilled vegetables.

The service can be slow and somewhat casual, but the food is good. Prices range from $3.50 for a mixed green salad to $13.50 for a full dinner entree.

55+ Seats • Beer and wine • Tight wheelchair access Metered parking and private park-and-lock lots nearby • Smoking permitted in designated area
Credit cards: **VISA M/C Diner's Club**

BRAD'S SWINGSIDE CAFE

Location:	4212 Fremont Avenue, Seattle
Phone:	633-4057
Days/Hours:	Dinner: Tues-Sat 5:30-10
	Brunch: Sat-Sun 8am-2pm
Reservations:	Accepted only for parties of 6 or more

Good jazz fills the air, and a genial host seats me happily at a window table. Conversation from the kitchen mixes with that of the customers. What Brad's Swingside lacks in polish it more than makes up for in good, substantial food and charm and character.

An exhuberant fan of baseball and swing-era jazz, owner Brad Inserra hung the walls of his ristorante with vintage black and white photos of baseball and jazz greats (hence the name Swingside). He carved out "the Grotto" in the back of his cafe for parties of six or more from a greenhouse. "I could just imagine this space with fish in it," he says, "so I draped it with fish nets and little fish lights, and painted fish on the walls." His food expresses the same ingenuity and from-the-heart character.

Brad was raised by first-generation Sicilians and Tuscans in Pennsylvania. Although I think the unrefined Sicilian style dominates, his food is an expression of both cuisines. He is not shy about using flavors he likes. Olive oil is infused with garlic and the heat of red peppers and tossed with pasta to make his memorable *Pasta Aglio Olio* with capers, anchovies, sun-dried tomatoes and lemon ($8.50). The swordfish special was marinated in the *aglio olio* along with herbs, lime and marsala and grilled ($13.95). A permanent menu offering of Moroccan Lamb Stew is his Sicilian grandfather's recipe ("Morocco is just a stone's throw from Sicily," says Brad). Entrees are $8.95-$14.95, and salads are a la carte, except for daily "hotsheet" specials.

55 Seats • Beer and wine • Tight wheelchair access Free on-street parking • No waiting area • No smoking • *Credit cards:* **VISA M/C Local checks**

BUONGUSTO

Location:	2232 Queen Anne Avenue N., Seattle
Phone:	284-9040
Days/Hours:	Lunch: Tues-Fri 11:30-2
	Dinner: Tues-Thurs 5-10, Fri-Sat 5-11
Reservations:	Requested for dinner

Owners Salvio and Anna Varchetta and Salvio's brother Roberto opened Buongusto in late 1990. Their Neapolitan origins clearly influence the menu: dash and style mixed with earthiness, freshness and spontaniety.

This home-now-restaurant at the top of Queen Anne Hill is one fine little place to eat. Arched interior stucco walls, plenty of natural light, tiled floors and a big sideboard loaded with antipasti and homemade desserts greet you. (Be advised, though, that these hard surfaces can create a noisy environment.) Seating extends under umbrellas to the outdoor terrace when weather permits.

The one-page lunch menu features antipasti, soups, salads and dolce — all á la carte. Lunch entree prices range $6.95-$8.25, with the "fish of the day" special generally around $10. The dinner menu expands to two pages and entree prices are $9.25-$17. The summer menu adds two fish specials per day and more salads. As Salvio says, "We know what we do best, and our customers count on having their favorite dish." Roberto's cooking is distinct, straightforward and wonderfully balanced.

When I dined there, the house wine was a Montepulciano (about $4 a glass). Count on Salvio or Anna to make an educated recommendation from their simple but excellent wine list. Prices are $18-$45; a "reserve" list is available.

75 Seats • Full Bar • Tight wheelchair access
Tiny waiting area • Free parking on adjacent streets
No smoking • *Credit cards:* VISA M/C AmEx

CAFE JUANITA

Location: 9702 NE 120th Place, Kirkland
Phone: 823-1505
Days/Hours: Mon-Sat 6-9:15, Sun 5:30-9:15
Reservations: Required

Cafe Juanita is not to be missed, however: (1) make reservations, and (2) get specific directions (it's a tough place to find). Little debate exists around the fact that Cafe Juanita is a culinary legend in this area. And while the restaurant itself is a lovely little upscale bistro set amidst trees and foliage just a few blocks from Lake Washington, the food is the raison d'etre.

As with so many of the best Italian restaurants, there is no set menu. You are served what Chef Chris Meldrum deems is freshest and in season. Among the blackboard specials the evening we were here were Lasagne ($13.25), a sausage-onions-peppers combination called *Spiedini Misti* ($14.25), and *Pollo con Panna e Carciofi* ($14.75), chicken and artichoke hearts with pasta in a rich savory cream sauce. Even small touches like their own freshly baked bread and vegetables served family-style augment the overall quality of dining here. Our broccoli and carrots were perfectly cooked, laced with shredded parmesan cheese and a bit of lemon. A wood-burning fireplace adds a backdrop of warmth and gaiety to the entire experience.

The wine list features a page of "Selezione della Casa:" wines of exceptional value and classic examples of each wine and region. The entire list is done by type (i.e., Orvieto, Pinot Grigio) with suggestions as to the foods they best complement. The server is most willing to assist you with your choices.

60 Seats • **Wine and Beer** • **Wheelchair access**
Free parking in adjacent lot • **Waiting area**
Smoking in designated area • *Credit cards:* **VISA**
M/C Local checks

CAFE LAGO

Location:	2305 24th Avenue E., Seattle
Phone:	329-8005
Days/Hours:	Lunch: Tues-Sun 11:30-2
	Dinner: Sun-Thurs 5-9, Fri-Sat 5-10
Reservations:	Not accepted

Cafe Lago is as true an expression of eating "Italian" as I have found in Seattle. It is a "must go" if you are serious about real Italian food. The owners are the cooks at this small bistro, the food reflects the season, the menu changes twice a week and the wine choices are superb.

Owners/chefs Jordi and Carla Viladas and Jordi's mother Angeline Viladas opened Cafe Lago in October 1990. Each cooks what he/she does best — and they do it with inspiration and natural talent. The sausages and pasta are their own; the Tuscan-style pizza is wood-fired; freshness is an imperative. As in Italy, fresh vegetables are found in abundance on the menu: ravioli filled with swiss chard, spinach, and ricotta and Parmesan cheeses, or lasagna layered with eggplant, bechamel, ricotta or tomato sauce. Three kinds of gnocchi — tomato, ricotta, and spinach — served with three cheeses appeared on a recent menu.

Dinner entrees hover around $11. You will find a superb assortment of antipasti ($4-$12.95). The wine list features local and Italian wines at $15-$40 a bottle, with a special Barolo list for the serious consumer priced at $45-$75 a bottle. Just ask your server to see it. Several delightful desserts are always be offered. The tiramisu is memorable!

56 Seats • Beer and wine • Wheelchair access
Free parking on numerous side streets • No waiting area • No smoking, please • *Credit Cards:* **VISA M/C AmEx**

CAFFE ITALIA

Location:	2448 76th Ave. SE, Mercer Island
Phone:	232-9009
Days/Hours:	Lunch: Tues-Fri 11:30-3
Dinner:	Tues-Thurs 5-9:30, Fri-Sat 5-10, Sun 4:30-9:30
Reservations:	Accepted

Caffe Italia is a sweet little ristorante set amidst insurance offices and hair salons in a low-rise office complex off a busy main thoroughfare in Mercer Island. Interior yellow walls are painted to simulate a courtyard in a countryside setting, and cozy nooks combine with open seating to create a warm, casual ambiance. (Is this *faux-rustic* in Mercer Islandese?) A second, smaller, dining room contains a wine bar, and outdoor seating in nice weather is bounded by a lattice fence and foliage.

The menu is primarily well-prepared standard Italian fare: antipasti for $2.95-$6.95 include *suppli al telefono* (breaded and fried rice balls filled with mozzarella cheese and served with marinara sauce). Salads and soups are $3.25 for mixed greens to $7.50 for marinated chicken with grilled eggplant. "Specialita Della Casa" are a variety of entrees for $6.95-$13.95 made with chicken, beef, veal and scampi; add $1 for soup or salad. Linguini and fettuccini are combined with Bolognese, marinara, puttanesca and Alfredo sauces.

Caffe Italia's easy charm and accessibility make it a perfect place for Islanders to meet for lunch or dinner.

90 Seats • **Wine and beer** • **Wheelchair access**
Free parking in adjacent lot • **Small waiting area**
Smoking in designated area • *Credit cards:* **VISA**
M/C Local checks

CALABRIA

Location:	132 Lake Street, Kirkland
Phone:	822-7350
Days/Hours:	Tues-Sun 5-10:30
Reservations:	Accepted

Calabria is tucked back off Lake Sreet in a small brick building. A tiny patio ringed with potted petunias invites outdoor seating in nice weather, and the warmth of the "Italian village" decor inside beckons in cold months. Increasingly popular with the Kirkland-Bellevue crowd and a growing number of Westsiders, this casual little trattoria is a great place for families and friends to gather for dinner.

The two-page menu offers antipasti (the Calamari Marinati is a strong favorite) for $4.25-$7.95. Pasta choices include standards like fettuccine Alfredo, manicotti, spaghetti puttanesca and spaghetti with tomato and mussels. You can order wonderful alternatives like fusilli caprese (fusilli tossed with fresh tomato, basil, mozzarella and parmesan) and ravioli ai funghi (ravioli with fresh mushrooms, cream and butter). The flavors are original, assertive and well-balanced. All pastas come with a salad and are priced $8.95-$10.75.

Main entrees of chicken, pork, veal and beef are also served with a salad and are priced $11.25-$13.95. Half portions are available for children. Five choices of pizza are available for $6.25-$7.95. Calabria has a superb zabaglione for dessert, one of the few I've found while researching this guide.

Red wines dominate the one-page wine list, and Chianti or Montelpulciano are available by the glass for $3.75, a good opportunity to try either. Bottle prices range $14.50-$50.

48 Seats • Beer and wine • Tight wheelchair access
Free parking on adjacent streets and in front lot
No waiting area • Smoking in designated area
Credit cards: **VISA M/C Local checks**

CELEBRITY ITALIAN KITCHEN

Location:	315 Second Avenue, Seattle
Phone:	467-1111
Days/Hours:	Lunch: Wed-Sun 11:30-2
	Dinner: Wed-Sun 5-10, bar service and
	food window until 2 am
Entertainment:	Deejays play different music genre
	starting 9 pm nightly; call for details.

Dancing every night to Old Faves or Techno Rave, good drinks and an easy Italian-inspired menu of pizzas, pastas and salads, make the Celebrity Italian Kitchen a place to come if you're in the mood to cut loose and unwind. The worn chairs and table tops indicate that a *lot* of people have done just that.

This is a *big* place. Bands of red neon ring the base of the balcony surrounding the dance floor, and there are stand-up bars, as well as tables and chairs. The walls are painted with scenes of Roman country estates, but they are barely visible in the dusky light. The lunch and dinner menu are the same and offer the usual pizza and pasta selections: fettucine Alfredo, four cheese tortellini, spinach and pesto tortellini. When you want to cast your cholesterol concerns to the four winds, order lobster agnolloti (lobster-stuffed egg pasta with both marinara and alfredo sauces). Prices are $6.95-$9.50. They claim to offer "the original first pizza ever" (I'm not sure what that means) of fresh roma tomatoes, basil and oregano, and a light coating of olive oil and mozzarella cheese for $6.95. The 15 pizza selections are $6.95-$8.95.

465 Seats • Full bar • Easy wheelchair access
Parking in adjacent nearby lots and on-street
Large waiting area • Smoking in designated areas
Credit cards: **VISA M/C AmEx**

CIAO BELLA RISTORANTE

Location:	25th Avenue NE, Seattle
Phone:	524-6989
Days/Hours:	Lunch: Mon-Fri 11:30-2
	Dinner: Mon-Thurs 5-10, Fri-Sat 5-10:30
Reservations:	Accepted for groups of 4 or more

Ciao Bella offers a warm and happy respite from the mayhem of traffic or a Northwest downpour. In a small building that once may have been someone's home, heavenly aromas of sweet basil and tomato and amber lighting give welcome contrast to busy 25th Avenue just east of the UW campus.

The food is decidedly southern Italian. Simplicity and authenticity are the watchwords. The evening I visited, the small bistro was filled with lively conversation, and chef/owner Gino Boriello appeared frequently to visit with patrons to be assured they enjoyed the dinners he had prepared. The wait staff seems to be thoroughly Italian and sometimes delightfully difficult to understand.

My companions ordered spaghetti puttanesca and linguini alle vongole, and I had the vitello capricciosa. Crusty bread dipped in garlicky olive oil is one of my favorites, and it's part of the standard presentation. Our meals were very good. Coffee, wine and the antipasto rustico were also excellent.

Entree prices range from $5.95-$12.75. The wine list is simple and features reds from the Piedmont, Tuscan, and Veneto regions. Bottles are priced $14.50-$56.

68 Seats • **Beer and wine** • **Tight wheelchair access**
Limited off-street parking in adjacent lot, free
on-street parking • **Comfortable waiting area**
Smoking in designated area • *Credit cards:* **VISA**
M/C Local checks

CUCINA! CUCINA!

Locations: 800 Bellevue Way, Bellevue, 637-1177
                   901 Fairview, Seattle, 447-2782
                   17770 Southcenter Pkwy, Tukwila,
                   575-0520
Days/Hours: Lunch: 11-4 daily
                   Dinner: Mon-Thurs 4-11, Fri-Sat 4-12,
                   Sun 4-10.
                   Bar hours (and a late night menu) vary
Reservations: Same day only; strongly advised

Certain adjectives come to mind whenever I enter a Cucina! restaurant: "hip," "slick," "with it." Each location conveys maximum sensory exposure to the latest trend in food and restaurant design. Schwartz Brothers Bill and John have given us a mass-market version of good Italian food, influenced by the northern style, that has popularized such notions as a bottle of olive oil on each table and Crayolas and butcher paper for fashionable doodling. Should you make a trip to the restroom, you'll hear an Italian language radio broadcast. What a touch.

Antipasti, soup, salads, pizza, pastas, bread and desserts (baked at Schwartz Brothers downtown) are priced for lunch from $2.25-$10. The dinner menu is an extended version of lunch, and entrees top out at $13.95. Wines are Italian and domestic, and the staff is well trained to make suggestions.

Cucina's chopped salad is locally famous, as are the oven-fired designer pizzas and antipasti selections. In my last visit, I sampled grilled prawns wrapped in pancetta and served with a very rich pesto-cream sauce. I recommend ordering the roasted elephant garlic; smashed and spread on bread it's divine!

180 Seats • **Full bar** • **Wheelchair access** • **Ample free parking** • **Waiting area** • *Credit cards:* **VISA M/C DISCOVER AmEx Local checks**

DaVINCI'S

Location:	89 Kirkland Avenue, Kirkland
Phone:	889-9000
Days/Hours:	Mon-Thurs 11:30-10:30,
	Fri-Sat 11:30 am-1:00 am, Sun 12-10:30
Reservations:	Not necessary
Entertainment:	Karaoke Wed-Thurs in bar, Fri-Sat in
	dining room.
	Dancing Fri-Sat in bar to Top 40 dee-jay

On a warm day you can walk up to DaVinci's from the Kirkland marina and find all the floor-to-ceiling windows tucked up against the ceiling. This, plus the patio seating, creates an indoor-outdoor atmosphere, a la the Mediterranean. Inside, vivid blasts of purple, green, yellow and red splash along the walls, table tops and floors. DaVinci's is a popular gathering place for a younger crowd, and the ambiance and prices suggest that families, especially ones with teenagers, will feel at home.

Made-to-order 10-inch and 14-inch pizzas are the main fare — 25 choices in all — priced $11.75-$17.95 for the 14-inch size. They prepare dough, sauces, and smoked meats daily on premises, using only fresh herbs. Pasta entrees ($7.95-$9.50) include the usual selections: lasagna, Alfredo, carbonara, primavera, and spaghetti and meatballs among them. Salads ($4.50-$4.95) and sandwiches (4.95-$5.95) round out the menu.

Wall-mounted televisions ring the dining room and bar so fans may cheer the hometown fellas during game times (many Seahawks and Sonics players live in Kirkland). Top 40 music keeps the place upbeat. If you really get caught up in the experience, you can even buy a DaVinci's tee-shirt to wear home.

120 Seats (+90 in bar) • **Full bar** • **Easy wheelchair access** • **Free on-street parking** • **Smoking in designated areas** • *Credit cards:* **VISA M/C AmEx Local checks**

DOMANI

Location:	604 Bellevue Way, Bellevue
Phone:	454-4405
Days/Hours:	Lunch: Mon-Fri 11:30-2:30
	Dinner: Mon-Thurs 5:30-10,
	Fri-Sat 5:30-10:30, Sun 5:30-9:30
Reservations:	Advised for weekend dinner

You sit in casual-chic Domani and you know you are in Bellevue. The deep green walls contrast with the texture of washed cedar, glass and brick. Lighting is minimal, and the spacious dining room is carefully divided into conversation areas so that there is a feeling of friendliness and intimacy for diners. A bar adjacent to the dining area is appointed with comfortable chairs and low tables. Domani is situated directly across the street from Bellevue Square. It is an ideal place for an upscale business lunch or dinner, or for enjoying a meal with friends.

The dinner menu offers antipasti, salads and 11 pasta selections (each served with a small mixed salad) all of which are traditional presentations--fettuccine Alfredo, spaghetti primavera, cannelloni al forno and manicotti con tre fromaggi (three cheeses). Pasta dishes are priced $9.25-$13.95. Meat entrees include Italian-inspired dishes made with chicken, prawns, veal and beef for $12.95-$16.95. The Saltimbocca alla Romana for $15.95 (scallops of veal sauteed with proscuitto, mozzarella and sage) is worth trying, and so is the Calamari San Remo (calamari with capers, garlic and tomato) for $13.95.

The wine cellar is a good mix of Italian and domestic; bottles range $14-$30, with specials by the glass for $3.50-$4.75.

70 Seats • Full bar • Tight wheelchair access
Limited free parking in adjacent lot • Waiting area
Smoking in designated area • *Credit cards:* VISA
M/C AmEx Local checks

FILIBERTO'S CUCINA ITALIANA

Location:	14401 Des Moines Memorial Dr., Burien
Phone:	248-1944
Days/Hours:	Lunch: Tues-Sat 11:30-3
Dinner:	Tues-Sat 5-10
Reservations:	Requested

In 1972 Mina and Ron Perry opened the legendary Filiberto's. Southern Italian roots influence the food. Mina and co-owner Natalina Genzale plan the menu and cook everything. They were one of the first in the area to import a machine from Italy and make their own pasta.

The dinner menu includes antipasti, soups, plenty of pasta selections, gnocchi, and selections of veal, chicken, fish, rabbit and beef. I chose the tortellini stuffed with veal and chicken served in a light tomato-cream sauce. Memorable! Prices are $6.50-$16; children's plates are available. Lunch consists of antipasti, fish, "house favorites" of salads, sandwiches, pizzas and calzoni. Prices are $4.75-$8.50.

A number of wine selections are sold by the class or carafe. If you want your own bottle, you select one from open stock on display. Bottles are priced, and the choices are superb. They have Barolos, Barbarescos, Nebbiolos, Chiantis, Dolcettos, and some good whites like Trebbiano, Orvieto, and Muscatos.

The restaurant is spacious and unpretentious. At its heart is a large, open kitchen where patrons amble back to chat with Mina and Natalina. An outdoor courtyard with adjacent bocci ball court is off the back dining room. Ron runs competitions throughout the good weather months.

180 Seats • Full bar • Easy wheelchair access • Free parking in adjacent lot • Children welcome • Smoking in designated area but no pipes or cigars, please
Credit cards: **VISA M/C AmEx Local checks**

GAMBARDELLA'S PASTA BELLA

Location:	1313 West Meeker Street, Kent
Phone:	859-4681
Days/Hours:	Lunch: Mon-Fri 11-5, Sat 12-5
	Dinner: Mon-Thurs 5-8:30, Fri-Sat 5-9
Reservations:	Recommended after 7 pm daily

Good Italian food *can* be found in a shopping mall. Opened in August 1991 by Matt and Alice Gambardella and their partner Hugh Golden, this restaurant is slowly being discovered. It is patterned after their highly successful venture in, of all places, Fairbanks, Alaska.

Fresh pasta (all flat pastas that can be rolled out are made in their kitchen), their own sausages, bread that is the best we have eaten in this area, Alice's homemade cheesecakes and wonderfully complex red sauces are definitely worth the trip. At Hugh's suggestion, we tried the manicotti stuffed with ricotta and mozzarella cheeses and laced with his marinara sauce. We preceded the pasta with an antipasto of assorted Italian meats and cheeses and crisp salads. Accompanied by their bread, this was a simple and delectable meal! Dinner entree prices are $8.50-$14.95 and include homemade minestrone soup or a salad.

The lunch menu caters to people in the area who have a 45-minute lunch break. You may call ahead and order out a number of vegetarian dishes (cheese ravioli, eggplant or zucchini parmigiano, fettuchini Alfredo), a calzone, or a variety of salads. Prices are $3.95-$6.95. A small deli in the back of the restaurant sells breads, pastas, desserts, and other items. Bring home a baguette of bread!

**99 Seats • Beer and wine • Easy wheelchair access
Free parking • No waiting area • Children welcome
Smoking in designated area • *Credit cards:* VISA
M/C Local checks**

GASPARE'S RISTORANTE ITALIANO

Location: 8051 Lake City Way NE, Seattle
Phone: 524-3806
Days/Hours: Sun-Thurs 5-10, Fri-Sat 5-10:30
Reservations: Not accepted

Gaspare's is a very popular little restaurant tucked off Lake City Way almost in Lake City. Since there are just 32 seats and they do not accept reservations, it's a good idea to call ahead to see if you will be able to get a table. Gaspare's is a cozy trattoria where you may dine in casual summer shorts or in business clothes after work. Mismatched chairs and tables crowded into a tiny space and fishing nets and strings of garlic draped here and there give it a delightful ambiance. That same familiar Italian tenor sings opera from a tape deck somewhere in the back of the restaurant.

The menu includes antipasti, six kinds of pizza, chicken, veal, various pastas and fish specials, depending on what's fresh and in season. Pizzas are $7.50-$9.95, and entree prices range $7.50-$14.95. The Risotto Ischitana (scallops, clams, mussels, calamari and prawns) takes its inspiration from a tiny island off the coast of Naples. The evening we ordered it, it was wonderful. Southern Italian (even Sicilian?) influences of lemon, marsala and red peppers are evident in their recipes. You'll find a hot-sweet combination at work in the marinara sauce and in the penne con salsiccia.

The wine list features Italian white wines from $16-$20 and Italian reds for $14-$30. Two selections of each are offered by the glass for around $4.

32 Seats • Beer and wine • Tight wheelchair access
Free on-street parking • Small waiting area
No smoking • *Credit cards:* VISA M/C

GENE'S

Location:	212 South Third Street, Renton
Phone:	271-7042
Days/Hours:	Lunch: Tues-Fri 11-3
	Dinner: Tues-Thurs 5-9, Fri-Sat 5-10
Reservations:	Recommended on Friday and Saturday

This little treasure of a place has been a well-kept secret in Renton for six years. Gene Sens is the chef, and he describes his menu as Italian "inspired." Delicious, dense baguettes (the denseness comes from olive oil) unlike anything you'll find in the region, fettucini tossed with sweet sundried tomatoes and artichokes, a variety of homemade stuffed raviolis and antipasti are, in my opinion, "inspired Italian!"

Cozy tables for two and four are found upstairs and down. When the weather turns warm, more tables are set on the front terrace, giving this house-turned-restaurant a festive air. Gene's two-page dinner menu includes appetizers, salads, pasta, entrees and small-portion side orders. Prices are $6.95-$13.95. His lunch menu offers calamari, foccacia, salads and sandwiches for $4.95-$7.95. Portions are ample, and the service is friendly and excellent. Finish your meal with a slice of one of their homemade cheesecakes, fruit pies, or tortes and accompany it with Caffe Mauro.

One thing in particular stands out at Gene's: there is no Italian tenor singing on tape. Instead, a classical guitarist serenades us from the tapedeck as we sip our house Montepulciano and savor Gene's superb bread. It's a nice change. Renton, you're in luck.

**100+ Seats • Beer and wine • Wheelchair access
Free parking in adjacent lot • No waiting area
Smoking in designated area • *Credit cards:* VISA
M/C Local checks**

GIANCARLO RISTORANTE AND PIZZA

Location:	4624 SW 320th, Federal Way
Phone:	838-1101 or 927-1510
Days/Hours:	Lunch: Mon-Sat 11-4
	Dinner: Mon-Thurs 4-10, Fri-Sat 4-11,
	Sun 4-10
Reservations:	Requested
Entertainment:	Live jazz with vocals Wed and Sat 7-10

Giancarlo's is nestled in a tiny shopping center. Owner/chef Peppe Napo and staff serve up superb pizza and fresh southern Italian food to adjacent suburban neighborhoods. All manner of style and dress are welcomed by Peppe as he greets and seats customers. Clientele in sweats and windbreakers form a steady line at the gleaming black and white tile bar for take-out pizza, stromboli, and calzone. Two nearby four-foot high stacks of pizza boxes are testament to the popularity of Giancarlo's creations, which range from $6.50-$15.95.

In the words of a fellow food fan, "Those pizzas are to die for!" The crust is laced with fresh garlic, the plum tomato sauce is homemade and all toppings are fresh and of the highest quality. Unless you're prepared to sip a glass of Chianti while you stand, call ahead for take-out.

The antipasti, pastas, veal, fish, and chicken are prepared in hearty southern Italian style are on the menu. The meats are excellent, the vegetables fresh, and sauces pungent and rich. Entree prices range from $11.50-$17.95 and include salad and bread. Live jazz on Wednesday and Saturday and a piano in the midst of diners invites amateurs to add their own music to the scene.

110 Seats • Full bar • Wheelchair access
Free parking in adjacent lot • No waiting area
Smoking in designated area (no pipes or cigars)
Credit cards: **VISA M/C Local checks**

GIUSEPPE'S

Location:	144-105th NE (the alley behind Ernst), Bellevue
Phone:	454-6868
Days/Hours:	Mon-Thurs 4:30-9:30, Fri-Sat 5-10
Reservations:	Advised for 4+ on weekends

Have you heard the expression "hole in the wall?" Giuseppe's *is* one, complete with green, white and red striped door, absolutely no natural daylight, smokey bar, Italian curios and bunches of empty straw-covered Chianti bottles hanging from the red-beamed ceiling. It's cozy, dark and slightly mysterious; if Giuseppe's were on Chicago's South Side, I'll bet men in fedoras would sit here and Make Plans. However, the many women, children and men who have been loyal customers of Giuseppe's since 1972 diminish the mysterious ambiance and add the gaiety and friendliness for which Giuseppe's is known. Booths for two and tables for four and six make this a nice place for families and couples to dine.

The menu appears to have steadily evolved over the years-- all six pages of it. Giuseppe's offers 26 combinations of pasta for $8.50-$12.95, which includes a bowl of their homemade minestrone soup or a trip to the salad bar. Chicken, veal and fish entrees are $13.95-$16.95, and pizzas with standard toppings like pepperoni, pineapple, and mushrooms are $11.95, plus extra for toppings for a 15-inch size. Fresh roasted garlic with the basket of bread is standard with all entrees.

The wine list is dominated by Italian wines for $14-$22 a bottle or $3.75 a glass.

70+ Seats • Full bar • Tight wheelchair access Small waiting area • Smoking in designated area; no pipes or cigars • Children welcome • *Credit Cards:* **VISA M/C AmEx Local checks**

GRAZIE

Locations: 3820 124th E., Bellevue, 644-1200
2301 N. 30th, Tacoma, 627-0231
16943 Southcenter Parkway, 575-1606
Days/Hours: Lunch: Mon-Sat 11-4
Dinner: Mon-Thurs 5-9:30,
Fri-Sat 5-10, Sun 4-9
Reservations: Requested evenings and weekends

Grazie restaurants are decidedly different in locale, size and ambiance, but certainly not in the high quality of the food they prepare. Owners Kevin Downey and Don Martelli are so determined to present authentic Italian food that they actually sent their executive chef and three head chefs to Italy to study the cuisine.

The Tacoma restaurant in Old Town commands a full view of Commencement Bay. It has a take-out deli with cheeses, meats, specially-roasted Grazie coffee and menu entrees. The Tukwila restaurant is hidden between a men's clothing store and a furniture store. The Factoria site (where the Arabica beans are roasted) is behind the Mall.

The presentation is primarily influenced by northern Italian style. The one-page lunch and dinner menus feature antipasti, soup (minestrone, of course), salads, veal, fish, chicken, and pasta. The pollo diavoli (broiled chicken with ricotta, proscuitto, pine nuts and red peppers) is superb, as is the capellini primavera (angel hair pasta with vegetables, garlic, and fennel). Lunches are $5.50-$8.95; dinners $6.95-$14.50.

The wine list consists of domestic and Italian selections with helpful explanations about what to expect of flavors and bouquet.

90+ Seats • Wine and beer • Wheelchair access
Ample free parking • Small waiting areas
Children's menu available • Smoking permitted in
designated area • *Credit cards:* VISA   M/C

IL BISTRO

Location:	93-A Pike Street (south end of Pike Place Market down and behind the newsstand)
Phone:	682-3094
Days/Hours:	Lunch: Mon-Fri 11:30-2 Dinner: Sun-Thurs 5:30-10, Fri-Sat 5:30-11
Reservations:	Recommended for weekend dinners

One of Seattle's enduring classic restaurants is tucked into a cobblestoned nook of the Pike Place Market, where parking is a pain and tourists walk unknowingly past. When you wander into Il Bistro, you are transported to a bistro that could be on a similar cobblestoned side street in Florence. The building is old enough not to feel like the walls and floors have had to be re-done to simulate "rustic." For an intimate dinner, ask for a table in the back of the room under the arch.

The hostess is congenial and knows good food, and chef Dino D'Aquila has designed a menu that will not disappoint. It features ten pasta dishes with choices like Penne con Melanzane (thinly sliced eggplant and fresh mozzarella with penne in a sweet tomato sauce) for $10.95, and Linguine Scampi alla Marinara for $15.95. Main course entrees include Cioppino for $19.95 and Frittura di Fileto (tenderloin sauteed with roast peppers and mushrooms and finished with red wine and cream) for $19.95. There are generally three or four nightly specials priced $10-$14.

The wine list is a good sampler of Italian and domestic wines. Prices are $20-$60, and various selections are available by the glass for $4.25-$6.50. Valet parking is available on Thursday, Friday and Saturday evenings.)

56 Seats + 40 in bar • Full bar • Wheelchair access
Metered and paid lot parking • Waiting area
Smoking in designated area • *Credit cards:* VISA
M/C AmEx Diners

IL PAESANO

Location:	5628 University Way NE, Seattle
Phone:	526-0949
Days/Hours:	Mon-Thurs 5-10, Fri-Sat 5-10:30
Reservations:	Suggested on weekends

Il Paesano is one of Seattle's perennial favorites. They've been dishing out wonderful Italian-style meals at this eatery since back when Ronald Reagan was president. (Kinda makes you a little sentimental, doesn't it?) The restaurant bears testament to customer loyalty to consistently good food, and it's one to seek out if you're in the mood for the eclectic U-District crowd and a hearty dinner.

Recently remodeled, Il Paesano is a tiny trattoria in the daylight basement of a house. The interior is cozy with arched ceilings and rustic terra cotta floors. In summer, its seating extends to an outdoor patio.

It is no accident that fish-loving Mediterranean countries hold squid in such high regard when it's prepared as well as Il Paesano's lemony Calamari Marinati. The Spaghetti Diavola (tiger prawns, garlic, and red pepper flakes) is also very good. The marinara sauce is slightly sweet and holds well to the spaghetti. Other menu items include veal, chicken and seven kinds of pizza. Prices are $8.25-$14.50. Salad comes with your dinner. Their wine list is very good, with about 35 red selections from which to choose starting at $8 a bottle. Wine by the glass is around $3.50.

32 Seats • **Wine and beer** • **Tight wheelchair access**
Free on-street parking • **Small outside waiting area**
Smoking in designated area • *Credit cards:* **VISA**
M/C Local checks

IL TERRAZZO

Location:	411 First Avenue S., Seattle
Phone:	467-7797
Days/Hours:	Lunch: Mon-Fri 11:30-3
	Dinner: Mon-Fri 5:30-10, Sat 5:30-10:30
Reservations:	Requested

When he opened Il Terrazzo eight years ago, owner Carmine Smeraldo carefully sculpted the space from a renovated Pioneer Square Building (Merrill Place) to achieve a feel of, in his words, "rustic elegance." Floor-to-ceiling draped windows let in maximum natural light during the day and open to an outdoor courtyard with textures and foliage that surround daytime diners with a sense of city and easy sophistication. In the evening the lighting and natural wood surfaces bring San Francisco to mind. If you are seeking a spot for an upscale business lunch or a romantic dinner for two, Il Terrazzo is your place.

Carmine's menu is a "fused" combination of Tuscan and Neapolitan influences with noteworthy fish preparation. We overheard raves about the halibut from diners at a nearby table. I chose an antipasto of Carpaccio con Garciofi (paper thin roast beef drizzled with olive oil and garnished with artichokes, fresh lemon, and parsley), and it was magnificent. Lunch entrees range from $6.50-$10.95, and dinner prices are a hefty $12.95-$24.50.

The wine list is extensive; and unless you have a working knowledge of the differences among French, Italian, and Northwest wines, I recommend that you focus on "Special Selections" listed on the first page. Dominated by good Italian reds, it simplifies the ordering process. Prices vary from $19 to $135 for an '85 Brunello di Montalcino.

90 Seats • Full bar • Easy wheelchair access
Parking in private lots and metered-on street • Small
waiting area • Smoking in designated area
Credit cards: **VISA M/C AmEx Diners Carte Blanc**

ITALIA

Location: 1010 Western Avenue, Seattle
Phone: 623-1917
Days/Hours: Lunch: Mon-Fri 11:30-2
          Dinner: Mon-Thurs 5-9, Fri-Sat 5-10,
          Sun (from July 4-Nov 25 each year) 5-9
          Deli is open Mon-Fri 7-8, Sat 10-8
Reservations: Requested for dinner

When you walk into Italia you are greeted by the comforting fragrance of sizzling olive oil and garlic, of roasting vegetables, of fresh herbs. The concept of quick, stylish food served cafeteria style by day and sophisticated dining by night has thrived for eight years in this polished uptown grill. Co-owners Dave Holt and Paul Schell know how to cater to their customers.

At 5 o'clock, Italia shuts down the fast-track cafeteria. The lighting dims, candles are set on the tables, and a full-service bistro emerges. Buttoned-down captains of industry dine elbow-to-elbow with chic art gallery owners or tourists who wander in from the waterfront a block away. The menu includes antipasti, pizza or calzone, salads and decidedly northern Italian pastas, risottos, and entrees of pork, fish or beef. Head chef Scott Craig confers regularly with managing partner Holt on the menu, which is changed to take advantage of seasonal foods. Domestic and Italian wines are carefully selected to pair with meals, and the prices are exceptional bargains. Dinners are $7.95-$12.95.

During the day, Italia is a shopper's delight. Baskets, retail wines, books, cards, and designer foods (pastas, polenta mixes, preserves, and olive oils) are for sale. You can dash in and take out a pasta salad, an espresso or daily specials and standard offerings of pizza, calzone, soups and salads ($2.25-$7).

**280 Seats • Beer and wine • Wheelchair access
Parking in private lots or metered spaces • Smoking in
designated area • *Credit cards:* VISA   M/C   AmEx**

ITALIAN GARDENS

Location:	1309 Auburn Way N., Auburn
Phone:	735-9464
Days/Hours:	Lunch and dinner: same menu.
	Mon-Fri 11-8:30, Sat 4-8:30
	If it's not busy, the restaurant closes
	Call ahead after 7 pm
Reservations:	Not necessary

When I sat down in Nick's Italian Gardens, I had the sensation that I was in one of those little pasta joints in an Idaho ski resort town: open fire pit, beer on tap, and Marilyn Monroe posters everywhere. Owner Nick Anagnos opened his restaurant in August 1991, and his "Italian niche" is to introduce authentic versions of midwest-style Italian food to us Northwesterners.

Just what would Yogi Berra order on a Saturday night in his hometown of St. Louis, anyway? For starters there are Chicago-style sandwiches — great big ones stuffed with meat balls or salami and provolone cheese and lots of red sauce. Or there's thin-crusted pizza topped with your choice of pepperoni, vegetables, and piles of cheese. Or how about rigatoni or fettucini heaped with tomato-meat sauce and cheeses? There's red sauce throughout the menu, so if you're partial to it, this is your place. Nick also features a St. Louis Italian Chili that is served over pasta and an Italian reuben sandwich. (The consequences of eating those creations do give one pause.)

The big-screen TV and pizza and sandwiches on weekends is perfect for this location. It's a fine spot for families or an after-softball team gathering place. Service is friendly, as are the prices: $5.25-$9.25. Add $1.25 each for salad or soup.

100 Seats • Beer and wine • Easy wheelchair access
Free parking • Children welcome • Waiting area
Smoking in designated area • *Credit cards:* VISA
M/C Local checks

JAY-BERRY'S

Location:	385 NW Gilman Blvd., Issaquah
Phone:	392-0808
Days/Hours:	Mon-Thurs 11-10, Fri 11-11,
	Sat 12-11, Sun 4-10
Reservations:	Accepted

Jay-Berry's has been in business just outside Gilman Village for over 10 years. This casual restaurant is known for excellent pan pizzas, house specials like fettuccine tossed with fresh vegetables, cheeses and traditional sauces like Alfredo and carbonara, big Caesar salads with Jay-Berry's own dressing and baked pastas like cannelloni and lasagne. Add to the substantial food a great bar and an exquisite setting on Issaquah Creek in Gilman Village, and you have the combination for their success.

The pizza dough and sauce are made fresh daily in their kitchen. Extra sauce is free, and you may create your own 10-inch pizza for $6.95 or your own 14-inch pizza for $11.95. If you don't feel especially creative, you may order one of their "House Specials" for $18 for the 14-inch size. "Sauteed Fettuccine" dishes are $9.75-$11.50 (I would not want to clean their saute pans with all that cheese!), and a variety of baked pasta are $9.50-$10.95. If you're not in the mood for Italian, but your friends are, you may order a grilled steak or pork chop or seafood for $9.95-$12.95.

Jay-Berry's is a fine place to stop after shopping in adjacent Gilman Village or to bring the family for a casual dinner. The wrap-around windows front Issaquah Creek, and the service is excellent. The bar has its own seating (and deck) and light menu of appetizers, soups and salads and hot sandwiches.

120 Seats + 30 in bar • Full bar • Easy wheelchair access • Free parking in surrounding lots • Waiting area • Children welcome • Designated smoking area • *Credit cards:* VISA M/C DISC Local checks

LA DOLCE VITA

Location:	3428 NE 55th, Seattle
Phone:	523-3313
Days/Hours:	Lunch: Mon-Fri 11:30-2
	Dinner: Mon-Sat 5-10
Reservations:	Requested, especially on weekends
Entertainment:	Live Italian opera on weekends, periodic violin soloists

Nestled in a tiny retail cluster at the southern edge of Seattle's Wedgewood neighborhood, La Dolce Vita has the feeling of a well-appointed country inn with its glazed tile floors, bronze statuary, richly laden wood sideboards and opulent bouquets of dried flowers. You can enjoy the Italian tenor on tape, or the live version serenading patrons on weekends after 7:30.

The lunch menu includes antipasti, insalate, zuppa, pasta, *carne* (meats), *pesce* (fish) of the day and *dolci*. Prices are $3.95 for a bowl of soup to $9.50. The dinner menu expands on lunch with prices for entrees ranging $9.50-$17.95. Patrons may also choose a five-course dinner for $22.95 per person, or a six-course dinner for $30.95 per person. Thursday nights all pasta is $7.75. I tried the Risotto Sorrentina with calamari, scallops and mussels, a spicy concoction that is on both lunch and dinner menus. The heat comes from flakes of red peperoncino, and it was very good.

The straightforward wine list features all reds and a few whites from Italy ($18-$45 a bottle) with several riservas ($50-plus). It's an excellent list. The servers can offer advice.

La Dolce Vita is owned by Raffaele Calise and Stefano Williams. Calise also owns Salute and Salute In Citta.

65 Seats • **Beer and Wine** • **Tight wheelchair access**
Free on-street parking • **Small waiting area**
No smoking • *Credit cards:* **VISA M/C Entertainment '92 cards Local checks**

LOFURNO'S

Location:	2060 15th W. (corner of Boston & 15th) Seattle
Phone:	283-7980
Days/Hours:	Wed-Sun 5pm-2am
Reservations:	Advised for weekend dinners
Entertainment:	Live piano jazz or blues on Sundays. Call for details.

This tan clapboard place with the lace curtains and paned windows would fit perfectly outside Providence, Rhode Island. (If you've never eaten Italian food in New England, do it. Forget New York or Chicago...) Lofurno's is like so many places I discovered in Rhode Island and Massachusetts, only it's much bigger in scale. And, to a certain degree, the food here is also of that southern Italian style found in New England.

The set menu is posted on a brass plate outside the front door (no deviations here!). It's very traditional: veal, seafood, pasta, chicken, or a special of the house of soup, salad, pasta, veal or chicken marsala, and spumoni for $19.50. Prices range $11.50-$16.50, all of which makes Lofurno's a perfect place to bring the grandparents or favorite relatives for a hearty, predictable Italian dinner.

The house salad is famous all over the city for its freshness and liberal use of Gorgonzola cheese. The bar is terrific "old-style" where you can come and stir your martini, think your thoughts, and listen to first-rate piano jazz and blues, while the lace curtains flap in the open window breeze. "Vintage" is as apt a descriptor as there is for Lofurno's.

230 Seats • Full bar • Wheelchair access from Boston Street • Waiting area • Parking on side street and in lot on Boston Street • Smoking in designated area • *Credit cards:* VISA M/C AmEx Local checks

LOMBARDI'S CUCINA

Location:	2200 NW Market St., Ballard, 783-0055
	729 NW Gilman Blvd., Issaquah, 391-9097
Days/Hours:	Lunch: Mon-Fri 11-3
	Dinner: Mon-Thurs 5-9:30, Fri-Sat 5-10
	Sun 5-10; Brunch: Sun 9-2:30
Reservations:	Advised but not required

Lombardi's originally opened in Ballard in 1987, but my travels took me to Issaquah to lunch at their much newer second location. It's a casual, well-run, well-appointed restaurant that serves very good Italian food with friendly service and pride. It's become a popular destination for Eastside families. A decorative visual barrier of masks and garlic bulbs hung with colorful ribbon streamers in the main dining room integrates three things for which Lombardi's is famous: their September Garlic Festival, a February two-week "Carnivale" and Ribbons Pasta Company.

I noticed right away that regular customers knew to ask for roasted garlic with the bread basket — it's standard at dinner, but lunch customers must ask. The dinner menu features antipasti and salads for $4.25-$7.50, a choice of seven pizzas for $6.50-$7.95, eleven traditional pasta selections for $8.95-$12.95. Poultry, meat and seafood entrees are $10.95-$14.95. Their pasta is made fresh daily; add $1 to all entrees for soup or salad. Lunch is a scaled-back version of dinner, with prices for salads, sandwiches, pasta and pizzas ranging $4.50-$7.50.

The desserts deserve mention: the cannoli, which part-owner and executive chef Neil Myles says was inspired by his Silician baker-grandfather; the crema caramellata by a neighboring diner was pronounced to be "perfect." The wine list is short but offers some very good Italian wines at $17-$30 a bottle.

95 Seats + 20 in bar • Full bar • Wheelchair access
Free parking in adjacent lots • Waiting area
Children welcome • Smoking in designated area
Credit cards: **VISA M/C Am Ex**

MAMMA MELINA'S

Location:	4759 Roosevelt Way NE, Seattle
Phone:	632-2271
Days/Hours:	Lunch: Mon-Fri 11:30-2
	Dinner: Sun-Thurs 5:30-10, Fri-Sat 5-10
Reservations:	Requested on weekends
Entertainment:	Live opera; call for specific dates/times

Mamma Melina's was opened several years ago by the talented Varchetta family who also own Buongusto. Big windows facinge busy Roosevelt Way scene and tables with very little space between them add to the feeling of barely controlled chaos. This is a fun, noisy place, especially when someone drops by to sing a little opera. The food and wine are first-rate.

Melina Varchetta is head chef, and most recipes are her family's from Naples — although I do think she's expressing a fused Italian style in some of the entrées. The mixed grill with sausage, chicken, lamb, vegetables and polenta squares, and the grilled herbed tomato on polenta were both stand-outs. Dinner entrées are $9-$17. Salads are á la carte at $2.50-$4. The desserts are excellent and priced around $3-$5 (portions are big enough to share). Bruschetta is served as you sit down, which is both good and bad: good because it's delicous, bad because one piece is all you get, and you can't order it as an appetizer.

Like Buongusto, Mamma Melina's wine list is excellent; and if you are unable to decide on a bottle, order the wine of the day. You can't go wrong. Wines by the bottle are $18-$35 with some specials slightly higher.

When the soloist arrives and begins to sing an aria while you feast on Mamma Melina's culinary creations, you know that you are, indeed, part of a very Full Life.

80 Seats • Beer and wine • Wheelchair access
On-street parking • No waiting area • No smoking
Credit cards: VISA M/C DISC Local checks

MIA ROMA

Location:	7614 Bothell Way, Kenmore
Phone:	486-6200
Days/Hours:	Mon 4-10, Tues-Thurs 4-11,, Fri-Sat 4-12, Sun 3-10
Reservations:	Accepted

From the Italian flag fluttering atop the red tile roof to the expansive outdoor dining courtyard covered with a canopy of grape vines laden with concord grapes, Teo's Mia Roma is the work of an artistic restauranteur. In business 19 years, Teo Di-Cicco is an artist at heart; in fact, his sculptures are in progress in the courtyard. But Mia Roma itself is Teo's most conspicuous piece of work. Depending on where you sit and your purpose for being there, it can be sprawling and noisy, or a discreet and familiar respite.

Mia Roma's two-page menu offers enduring Italian classics made with linguini, fettuccini and rigatoni, with nightly specials like lasagna ($10) or spaghetti ($9.50). Twenty-four pizza choices in 14-inch and 16-inch sizes are available for $12.50-$17 for the 16-inch size. "Specialita Italiana" are entrees ordered a la carte or as a full dinner with soup, salad, bread, and spumoni or vanilla ice cream. Prices for dinners are $11.60-$16.95. The portions are substantial, and the expansiveness of the hospitality and scale of Mia Roma make it worth the trip to eat here. The rustic feel of the stucco-enclosed courtyard is unlike any place else in Seattle.

400 Seats • Full bar • Wheelchair access • Free parking in adjacent lots • Waiting area • Smoking in designated areas • Children welcome • *Credit cards:* VISA M/C AmEx Diner's Carte Blanche Local checks

PALOMINO

Location:	Third Floor, Pacific First Centre, 5th & Pike, Seattle
Phone:	623-1300
Days/Hours:	Lunch: Mon-Sat 11:30-2:30
	Dinner: Sun-Thurs 5:30-10
	Fri-Sat 5:30-11
Reservations:	Recommended for lunch and dinner

While Palomino does bills itself as a "Euro-Seattle Bistro", the style of food here is clearly dominated by the northern Italian influence. I have always been impressed with the quality, substance and verve at work in the kitchen and throughout the entire restaurant. It is a place I do not hesitate to recommend to out-of-town business people, and it is one to which I readily invite acquaintances with an appreciation for sophisticated food.

From the street or parking garage, enter the stylish Pacific First Centre and go up to the third floor where Palomino occupies a dominant corner. The dinner menu consists of appetizers and salads ($2.95-$9.95), wood-fired pizzas ($5.95-$8.95), superb Palomino "Signatures" for $11.95-$17.95, pasta dishes ($7.95-$11.95), applewood grilled seafood or steak ($13.95-$18.95), and spit-roasted chicken, pork or duck for $12.95-$16.95. I recommend any of the spit-roasted meats and Palomino "Signatures," especially the cassoulet (a variety of meat slow-cooked with cannellini beans, garlic and brandy).

The wine list is excellent, with a number of Italian and domestic choices under $20 a bottle.

**200 Seats • Full bar • Elevator wheelchair access
Free parking in Pacific First Centre garage after 5 pm
weekdays and all day Saturday and Sunday • Waiting
area • Smoking in designated area • *Credit cards:*
VISA M/C AmEx DISC Local checks**

PAPA LUIGI'S

Location:	31406 Pacific Hwy S., Federal Way
Phone:	839-1333
Days/Hours:	Mon-Thurs 11-10:30, Fri-Sat 11-11:30, Sun 11-10
Reservations:	Accepted

Opened in June 1992, Papa Luigi's is one of the newest addition to Italian-inspired restaurants in Federal Way. Concertina music enhances an underlying suggestion of Old World briskness and animation, and a gregarious staff adds to the fun-loving ambiance. This is a place for people who want to let their hair down in an expansive, casual restaurant, and families are certainly included in this category. Butcher paper and crayons on each table invite "kids" to record missives from the evening and leave them for display on the walls, or take them home as personal souvenirs.

The menu is unique in several ways. "Create Your Own" pasta dishes for $5.95 each include a tossed salad and offer eight different pastas with seven traditional sauces like marinara, Alfredo, pomidoro, pesto and verde (nice mix of red and green). You choose your own combination. Lunch has an abbreviated selection for $3.75. All baked pastas are $7.95 ($4.75 for lunch). Also, Papa Luigi features *Turletti*, which is chicken ($8.95), steak ($9.95), or shrimp ($10.95), marinated in a "secret sauce" and sauteed with fresh vegetables and served with polenta and pasta. A kids' menu is available.

244 Seats • Full bar • Wheelchair access • Free parking • Waiting area • Designated smoking area Children welcome • *Credit cards:* VISA M/C AmEx Local checks

PASTA BELLA

Locations:	5909 15th Ave. NW, Seattle, 789-4933
	1530 Queen Anne Ave. N., 284-9827
Days/Hours:	Ballard: Mon-Sat 5:30-10, Sun 4:30-9:30
	Queen Anne: Lunch: Mon-Fri 11:30-4,
	Sat-Sun 12-4
	Dinner: Mon-Sat 4-10, Sun 4-9
Reservations:	Recommended

If you came from expressive Iranian-Italian parentage and had a passion for food, what would you do? David Rasti told his mother he wanted to be a dentist, left for the United States, and opened a resturant in Seattle. He arrived in Ballard about five years ago amidst cheers from the local food press, and Pasta Bella on Queen Anne debuted in June 1991.

While the Ballard restaurant is funky and Queen Anne is casual chic, they both share David's attention to detail and commitment to giving customers a great $15 meal. "Everything is cooked fresh," he says, "and we want our customers to be happy. We even babysit the kids." While some family-style Italian restaurants compromise their menus for "family fare," this is not the case at Pasta Bella.

The pastas are superb. They are cooked to a perfect *al dente* and then infused with the particular entree's sauce. I especially recommend the gorgonzola-walnut stuffed ravioli, the fettuccini con funghi, or the linguini con vongole. Dinner entrees range from $7.95-$12.95, and lunch prices are $5.95-$7.95. The wine list is simple and dominated by Italian reds, but also includes domestic choices. Put Pasta Bella on your "must go" list.

70 Seats • **Beer and wine** • **Free on-street parking**
Small waiting area • **Children welcome** • **Smoking**
in designated area • *Credit cards:* **VISA M/C DISC**
AmEx DINERS Local checks

PINK DOOR

Location:	1919 Post Alley, Seattle
Phone:	443-3241
Days/Hours:	Lunch: Tues-Sat 11:30-2:30
	Dinner: Tues-Sat 5:30-10
	Bar: Tues-Thurs until 12 am, Fri-Sat
	until 2 am, $3 cover on weekends
Reservations:	Requested
Entertainment:	Cabaret-style; from jazz to accordion

There's no sign but the door *is* pink and so are the bas-relief pillars on either side. Inside, bright plastic table cloths, metal tables and chairs and planked floors smoothed by years of heavy foot traffic recall the 1940's. Add live jazz or cabaret-style music, a plate of pasta, a glass of red wine, and you could be in a Humphrey Bogart movie. Outside, the trellis-covered veranda with its multi-colored lights, honeysuckle vines, and vista of the harbor always makes me feel I'm on Holiday.

When owner Jackie Roberts opened her restaurant in 1984, her European concept was a hit. The simple, "unprocessed" spontaneous culinary style quickly made the Pink Door a "must" in Seattle gustatory circles.

Dinner is a four-course meal for $17.50 that changes weekly. Courses include an antipasto, pasta, a choice of three entrees and a salad. Beverages and desserts are extra. Lunch includes the usual: antipasto, pasta, salads, fish and chicken specials, or pizza. Lunch entree prices are $5.50-$10. The food is predominately northern Italian-inspired. Breads are Brenner Brothers, and the coffee and espresso are SBC.

The wine list is a mix of Italian, French and domestic choices. Music and an á la carte menu are offered nightly in the bar. If you haven't been here yet, you must go to be "in."

60 Seats +60 in bar • Paid parking • No waiting area • Smoking in restricted area • *Credit cards:* VISA MC

PIZZUTO'S ITALIAN CAFE

Location:	5032 Wilson Ave., Seattle
Phone:	722-6395
Days/Hours:	Lunch: Mon-Fri 11:30-2
	Dinner: Mon-Sat 5-9
Reservations:	Recommended for evenings

Across the street from the Seward Park Puget Consumer's Cooperative, Pizzuto's is a comfortable neighborhood trattoria owned and operated by brothers Frank and Vince Pizzuto. It is also the *only* Italian restaurant on the west side of Lake Washington from Leschi south to Seward Park.

Vince is the main cook. His home-style recipes come from Mamma Pizzuto, who emigrated with her husband to the United States in 1956 from a small hilltop village east of Naples.

The lunch menu offers meatball or Italian sausage sandwiches served with soup or salad for $3.95-$5.95, salads or soup for $2.15-$4.50 and pasta served with soup or salad for $4.95-$5.95. Dinner entrees include pizza, pasta, veal, seafood, chicken and "homemade specialties" like ravioli, gnocchi and cannelloni di Maria. Prices are $7.95-$13.95 and include soup, salad and warm bread.

The staff is friendly, and the red and white checked table cloths, wooden pressback chairs, ceiling fans and musical background (songs like Dean Martin's rendition of "That's Amore") add to the delightful ambiance of this little trattoria. If you're in the neighborhood, stop in and order a plate of their gnocchi or a pizza.

50 Seats • Beer and wine • Easy wheelchair access Free on-street parking • Small waiting area • Children welcome • No smoking, please • *Credit cards:* VISA M/C Local checks

POGACHA

Location:	119 - 106th Ave. NE, Bellevue
Phone:	455-5670
Days/Hours:	Lunch: Mon-Fri 11:30-2:30
Dinner:	Tues-Thurs 5:30-9, Fri-Sat 5:30-
Reservations:	Advised for weekend dinners

I may be stretching geography a bit by including Pogacha in a guidebook of Italian restaurants. Pogacha is the name of a Croatian flatbread, and while the name and some menu items have Croatian roots, the style of food prepared here appeals to anyone with a taste for Italian food. (After all, Italy and what was once Yugoslavia do share a border and the Adriatic Sea.) Call it "Yugo-Italian" and take your friends. They'll thank you for it.

The one-page menu features chef's specialties, pasta, "Pogachas" (pizza-like creations made on pogacha) and salads. Specialties include marinated skewered lamb flavored with garlic and aromatic herbs for $9.95, braised lamb shanks with polenta ($9.95), and veal sauteed with roasted garlic and smoked tomatoes ($9.95). Specialties change regularly, but what you find will be of similar superb quality, price and imagination. Pogachas (compare the texture and taste to focaccia) come with an assortment of toppings like Italian sausage and Kalamata olives ($7.25), chicken, Gorgonzola and walnuts ($7.75) and fresh mushroom and pesto ($6.75). They draw raves!

The location isn't especially charming (a strip of small businesses), but the sleek white interior with its open kitchen and gleaming tiled ovens is. The service is friendly and competent.

A limited, but good, selection of California and Washington wines is moderately priced by the glass ($3-$4.25) and bottle (under $20.00).

65 Seats • Beer and wine • Wheelchair access
Free parking in adjacent lots • Small waiting area
No smoking • *Credit cards:* VISA M/C

POOR ITALIAN CAFE

Location:	2000 Second Avenue at Virginia, Seattle
Phone:	441-4313
Days/Hours:	Lunch: Mon-Fri 11-4
	Dinner: Mon-Thurs 4-10, Fri-Sat 4-11,
	Sun 4-9 (winter), 4:30-9:30 (summer)
Reservations:	Recommended

Was owner Gregory Pesce a poor Italian seven years ago when he opened this fine little bistro? Maybe so, but today the name is definitely in contrast to the upscale ambiance of exposed brick, yellow washed columns and fresh flowers on the tables.

The one-page lunch and dinner menus are nearly identical, except that the lunch menu offers several sandwich choices and fewer pasta and appetizer selections. An array of pasta dishes, salads, entrees and pizzas are available for $5.50-$8.95. They also serve daily specials. Dining here for the uninitiated may prove to be a challenge; there are no descriptions for menu items like "ravioli alla Nona" or "cappellini Stefano." My assumption is that these dishes are made the way Stefano or Nona makes them. If so, head chef Stephen Carter makes a dynamite dish of Capellini Stefano — a wonderful blend of artichokes, garlic, tomatoes, capers and onions served with angel-hair pasta.

This is an excellent place to have a business lunch or dinner in casual surroundings close to downtown, or to bring out of town visitors to show them that Seattle does, indeed, have some fine little Italian trattorias. The portions are large and I've never had a bad meal here.

**92 Seats • Beer and wine • Wheelchair access
Metered on-street parking before 6 pm • Small
bar/waiting area • Smoking in designated area but
no pipes or cigars, please • *Credit cards:* VISA M/C
DISC AmEx Local checks**

PORTOBELLO

Location:	30333 Pacific Highway S., Federal Way
Phone:	839-3700
Days/Hours:	Lunch: Mon-Fri 11:30-2:30
	Dinner: Mon-Thurs 5-10,
	Fri Sat 5-10:30, Sun 4-9
Reservations:	Recommended on weekends
Entertainment:	Karaoke, live music Fri-Sat 5-9 in bar
	Live jazz Sundays 5-9

Ristorante Portobello is situated in a big building that originally housed a seafood chain restaurant. Unfortunately the highly efficient air conditioning system eliminates many of the wonderful smells of chef Rosetta Genzale's creations and sneeze guards interfere with the display of fresh antipasti, desserts, and salads. You will, however, find the food much to your liking.

Rosetta's recipes come from her southern Italian heritage. My companion and I had gnocchi with pesto and spaghetti quattro frommagi. We found a lovely balance of flavors in each dish instead of the frequent heavy-handed use of garlic often present in similar preparations done by less skilled cooks. The menu is extensive and features plenty of seafood, pasta, chicken, veal, and oven-fired pizzas. Everything is homemade, including the gelato, and it's all a la carte. Entree prices range from $6.50-$15.95. Chef Rosetta chats and visits with guests as she pulls pizzas from the open-fired ovens, and it's obvious she enjoys her work.

Portobello is perfect for families; Sundays feature a "family style" dinner of rigatoni and meatballs for $8.95, with kids' portions at $5.95. The service is excellent. A background of live music in the bar during the evening makes this a nice place to unwind.

**236 Seats • Full bar • Easy wheelchair access
Free parking • Children welcome • Comfortable
waiting area • Smoking in designated area**
Credit cards: VISA M/C AmEx Local checks

RISTORANTE MACHIAVELLI

Location:	1215 Pine Street, Seattle
Phone:	621-7941
Days/Hours:	Dinner: Mon-Thurs 5-10, Fri-Sat 5-11
Reservations:	Recommended for weekends

I think Machiavelli's has some sort of "pasta karma," because when you walk by, you are literally compelled to go in. One person I know says that she goes there when she's down and in need of what she calls "pasta therapy." (She also goes there when she's happy.) Happy or sad, this friendly little spot up from downtown on the Capitol Hill side of Pine Street won't disappoint you.

Tom and Linda McElroy opened Machiavelli about four years ago. They've created a "we're all in this together" atmosphere, and it comes through in the noisy, friendly welcome and their willingness to accomodate your special requests. Basically, they want to feed you what makes you happy. Their menu features over 16 pastas dishes (surely one of them can comfort you) priced $7.75-$9.75. The Linguini alla Puttanesca is rich with capers and olives, and you can heat it up a bit with a shaker of hot pepper flakes if you're so inclined. The Fettucini Carbonara packs a lot of heat and garlic, and they do a marinara sauce for vegetarians.

The small, select pizza creations get rave reviews throughout the city and are priced $5.25-$5.75. Entrees with free-range veal and chicken are $10.95-$13.50. The homemade vanilla bean cheesecake could cure anyone's blues, and they have some fine selections of wine by the glass for $2-$5. Wines by the bottle are $12-$32 and include Italian and domestic choices.

44 Seats • Beer and wine • Tight wheelchair access
Free on-street parking • Small bar/waiting area
Smoking throughout • *Credit cards:* VISA   M/C
Local checks

RISTORANTE PARADISO

Location:	120 Park Lane, Kirkland
Phone:	889-8601
Days/Hours:	Lunch: Mon-Sat 11-2:30
	Dinner: Mon-Sun 5-10:30
Reservations:	Recommended for dinner

Amidst art and frame shops in trendy downtown Kirkland sits Ristorante Paradiso. Put this place on your "must go" list. Fabrizio Loi, a shy and talented chef from Sardinia, opened Ristorante Paradiso 1-1/2 years ago; this guy can cook.

The two-page lunch and dinner menus are imaginative and simple. Fabrizio favors a less pungent, more savory approach to Italian food. Crespelle Ricotta e Spinaci (green pasta crepes stuffed with spinach and ricotta cheese in a cream/tomato sauce), Penne Paradiso (artichoke hearts and pasta bathed in the same delicate tomato/cream sauce), or Saltinbocca alla Romana (veal, sage and proscuitto in a white wine sauce) are examples of what you'll find. Dinner prices are $8.95-$15.50. Lunches are $3.50-$10.95. Accompanying your meal is a round of Fabrizio's freshly-baked Italian bread. It's the real thing! The first bite of my Caesar salad told me he uses anchovies and egg yolks in his dressing (also the real thing).

Maitre d'-Sommelier Enrico Fabregas has built a wine cellar that is as comprehensive a collection of Italian wines as anyone offers to diners in this region. (The cellar also includes French and domestic wines.) Enrico is a nationally-ranked sommelier. Do take advantage of his good nature and willingness to share his enthusiasm for the grape! Get some friends to join you and have a regular tasting along with your Italian feast.

60 Seats • Beer and wine • Easy wheelchair access
Free on-street parking • Smoking in designated area
Small waiting area • *Credit cards*: VISA M/C
AmEx Local checks

RISTORANTE PONY

Location:	621-1/2 Queen Anne Ave., Seattle
Phone:	283-8658
Days/Hours:	Tues-Fri 5-11, Sat-Sun 5-12
	Brunch Sat-Sun 11-3
Reservations:	Strongly advised

The "one-half" designation of Ristorante Pony's address is also a clue to its physical size and location among the businesses at the base of Queen Anne Hill. It's a tiny gem of a place with a "Euro-Italian" menu, which simply means the chef has the latitude to fix anything inspired by cuisines from countries more or less adjacent to Italy. One evening you might find Syrian Lentil Soup, a Greek-inspired hummus plate with fresh vegetables and tsalziki yogurt, and an Italian entrée. Consider a visit to Ristorante Pony an opportunity to be an armchair culinary tourist.

Everything is á la carte, and the menu changes frequently. From the assortment of appetizers priced $4.25-$7.50, my companion and I shared an Eggplant Terrine (baked eggplant drizzled with anchovy butter and seasoned croutons) for $4.75. Salads are $3.25 for a mixed green salad to $7.95 for a rich mid-Eastern combination plate. Six pasta selections for $8-$10.95 were offered, and we chose a Penne Arrabiata ($8), (penne served with a sauce of roasted garlic, fresh tomato, arugula and mushrooms); it was delicate and delicious! From the sauté menu we chose a very rich Pollo Ripieno ($11.50) — a breast of chicken stuffed with roasted red peppers, provolone cheese, and coppa salami served with marinara sauce.

If you are adventuresome with food, Ristorante Pony is your place. Depending on the other 20+ people there with you that evening, the atmosphere can be intimate or animated.

35+ Seats • **Full bar** • **Tight wheelchair access**
Metered parking • **No waiting area** • **Smoking
permitted** • *Credit cards:* **VISA M/C Local checks**

RISTORANTE di RAGAZZI

Location:	2329 California Ave. SW, West Seattle
Phone:	935-1969
Days/Hours:	Lunch: Mon-Fri 11-2:30
	Dinner: Mon-Sun 4:30-1 am
	Brunch: Sat-Sun 8:30-2:30
Reservations:	Accepted only for 6+ people

I sat sipping a glass of Pinot Grigio, surrounded by bright yellow stencilled walls, green wicker furniture and aromas from the spacious open kitchen. It was a pleasant moment, indeed.

A lot of spit-and-polish went into creating this ristorante. If you want a casual dinner with friends or family, this is a place to choose. "Di Ragazzi", (Larry Denaro, John Denaro, Kenny De-Mile, and Rob Ross) have married a menu of traditional Italian entrees with tasteful decor and an atmosphere of freshness and vitality. Selections include an excellent assortment of antipasti for $2.95-$8.95 and pastas like Fettucini Pesto, Spaghetti Carbonara, Linguini alla Puttanesca. Pasta dishes are $6.95-$8.95. Chicken, veal and fish entrees served with a house salad or vegetables are priced $8.95-$13.95. They also offer seven kinds of 10-inch pizza for $6.95-$7.95. Kids are half-price for pizza and pasta dishes, and senior citizens receive a 10% discount.

The one-page wine list offers some good selections of well-known Italian labels and wine varieties. Prices range $14-$30.

For parties of 10 or more you may have your "own personal Italian chef to take care of you" in their Stanza di Famiglia (Family Room). Advance reservations are required.

99 Seats • Beer and wine • Easy wheelchair access
Free on-street parking • Ample waiting/bar area
Smoking in designated area • *Credit cards:* VISA
M/C AmEx Local checks

SALEH AL LAGO RISTORANTE

Location:	6804 Greenlake Way N., Seattle
Phone:	525-4044
Days/Hours:	Lunch: Mon-Fri 11:30-2
	Dinner: Mon-Sat 5:30-9:30
Reservations:	Requested/Recommended

Saleh Al Lago is the only restaurant from the Pacific Northwest to be nominated and inducted into the nation's Restaurant Hall of Fame. This sleek continental bistro offers a tranquil table, a cosmopolitan crowd and superbly crafted meals.

Chef Saleh Joudeh, Syrian by birth, is an instinctive cook whose style is influenced by the eight years he spent studying in Perugia, in the heart of Italy's Umbrian region. Although he came to Seattle to finish his medical studies, he worked in a restaurant, found his true calling, and met his future business partner, Dorothy Frisch.

Saleh's *nouvelle* style integrates ingredients like citrus, garlic, fresh vegetables, capers and freshly-made pasta. He uses just three meats: beef tenderloin, boneless chicken and lamb — and fresh fish. My spinach and ricotta-stuffed ravioli drizzled with butter and finely chopped garlic bits, and garnished with a spring of fresh sage was so fresh and so well prepared that I could taste the earthy edges of the flour as the dish unfolded deep, layered tastes of pungent cheese, sweet butter, garlic and sage.

Lunch prices are $8.50-$10.75. Dinner entrees are $12.75-$16.75. The wine list is a sampling of Italian, domestic and French. Bottle prices are $15-$50; by the glass, around $4.

66 Seats • Full bar • Wheelchair access on lower level • Small enclosed waiting area • Designated smoking are; no pipes or cigars • *Credit cards:* VISA M/C AmEx Diners Club Local checks

SALUTE

Location:	3410 NE 55th, Seattle
Phone:	527-8600
Days/Hours:	Tues-Sun 5-10
Reservations:	Not accepted

If you want to learn a few quick Italian words, this is a good place to practice. At Salute, they greet you, they seat you, they converse with each other, they quarrel, they say good bye to you — all in Italian. It's fast-paced. I can never tell if they are happy to see me, or if they just want to hustle me in and greet the next guest. This trattoria has hundreds of loyal customers who swear there's no better Italian food in Seattle.

Veal and seafood are the specialties. The chef is inclined to use pine nuts, almonds, pistachios, cream, butter, brandy and lemon in a variety of sauces with scallops and other seafoods, chicken, veal and pasta. It's wonderful, imaginative stuff. The cuisine is more reminiscent of Bologna than that served anywhere else in town. For that reason alone, I recommend you try Salute. Dinner entree prices are $8.50-$16; consistent with the originality at work in the kitchen, there are plenty of nightly specials from which to choose. It's worth noting that the price includes salad and bread. Study the blackboard and order something you've never tried before. Live on the edge.

There's no Italian tenor on tape (it's Tony Bennett and Dean Martin instead) and the experience of eating here is heightened by being seated in any one of a series of small rooms. Someday I'll learn enough Italian to ask what that overturned boat is doing on the ceiling.

65 Seats • Beer and wine • Wheelchair access • Free on-street parking • Tiny waiting area • Smoking permitted in designated area • *Credit cards:* **VISA M/C Local checks**

SALUTE IN CITTA

Location:	620 Stewart St. (Vance Hotel), Seattle
Phone:	728-1611
Days/Hours:	Lunch/Dinner: Sun-Thurs 11:30-10, Fri-Sat 11:30-11; Lunch and dinner are ordered from the same menu
Reservations:	Recommended
Entertainment:	Live jazz Thurs-Fri-Sat evenings 9 pm

The combination of live jazz and prime downtown location make this a popular gathering place. Table service is unobtrusive, the atmosphere is lively, and my five dining companions just flat-out enjoyed being at Salute in Citta. The quality of the food was clearly a secondary concern. It was crowded, noisy and fun, perfect for a festive night out with friends.

Each of us ordered a different menu item. Our choices included spaghetti marinara, a pizza, chicken with lemon and capers and fettuccine with scallops. All of us agreed that the cook was heavy-handed with the black pepper and that the balance of heat and garlic needed some attention. But we ate everything, including four baskets of Grand Central bread. The house Chianti was fruity and a good complement to the style of food presented. Entrée prices are $7.50-$15.50 and include salad.

Owner Raphaele Calese also operates Salute on NE 55th in Seattle, and local culinary opinion favors the food at the original restaurant.

100 Seats • Full bar • Tight wheelchair access
Parking in private lots and metered on-street
Small waiting area • Smoking in designated area
Credit cards: **VISA M/C**

SALVATORE RISTORANTE ITALIANO

Address:	6100 Roosevelt Way NE, Seattle
Phone:	527-9301
Days/Hours:	Dinner: Mon-Thurs 5-10, Fri-Sat 5-11
Reservations:	Not taken

In 1990, after numerous dinners at this once-quiet little corner trattoria, my husband and I arranged to meet friends at Salvatore for a leisurely evening. When we arrived, we were mightily disappointed to find the place jammed with other diners. Someone must have reviewed it in the local papers. It was no longer our own little find.

Happily fame hasn't spoiled Salvatore. The puttanesca packs a Sicilian wallop of anchovies and hot peppers, the carbonara sauce bathes the rigatoni in a smokey richness, and the veal, whether in lemon or with mushrooms, is sweet and fresh. The menu consists of antipasti, salads, soup, pizza, pasta and several fish and meat entrees. Prices are $7-$14.50. Salads are a la carte with pizza and pasta dishes. There are always several daily specials as well.

Salvatore has the ambiance of an interior grotto. It is darkly lit with tables close together, and prints of Italy hang on walls frescoed with grape vines. The crowd spills in from the surrounding Ravenna and Green Lake neighborhoods, many looking as if they just left a University of Washington research lab or classroom. Salvatore is a great place to go with friends, but be prepared to wait. They don't take reservations and it is crowded (and often noisy) even on week nights.

50 Seats • Beer and Wine • Wheelchair access
Free on-street parking • Small bar/waiting area
Smoking permitted at bar • *Credit cards:* VISA
M/C Local checks

SERAFINA

Location:	2043 Eastlake Ave. E., Seattle
Phone:	323-0807
Days/Hours:	Lunch: Mon-Fri 11:30-2:30
	Dinner: Sun-Thurs 5:30-10
	Fri-Sat 5:30-11
Reservations:	Recommended for dinner
Entertainment:	Piano, jazz, and vocals Tues-Sat with
	Mezzo items offered until 1 am

Serafina, with its tiny garden courtyard, concrete floors and deliberate rustic style, might well be nestled in the hills of Tuscany instead of the hill rising above the east side of Lake Union.

Owned and operated by Susan Kaufman and Lois Pierris, Serafina opened in May 1991. Both are native to Brooklyn and came to Seattle from distant parts of the world. Their combined culinary and artistic experiences are abundantly evident in Serafina's apt expression of northern Italian country cooking.

The lunch menu offers soup, grilled focaccia sandwiches (panini), several specials and salads. Prices are $3.75-$6.95. I sampled polenta layered with a heady Bolognese sauce laced with fennel and bits of gorgonzola. The dinner menu includes many of the lunch items with expanded "mezza" (their version of antipasti) courses, specials of chicken, lamb and prawns, and pasta rustica and risotto dishes. Prices for dinner entrees are $7.95-$14.95. Dinner hours are crowded and noisier than the relaxed lunch time atmosphere. Live music ("torch songs" and sultry female singers) is very popular.

The wine list is an eclectic collection of Italian, Greek, German, Chilean, and domestic wines, with some exceptional values. Bottles are priced from $11-$35; by the glass, $2.50-$4.50.

90 Seats + 35 outside • Full bar • Tight wheelchair access • Free parking • Waiting area Smoking area
Credit cards: **VISA M/C Local checks**

SIMPATICO

Location:	4430 Wallingford, Seattle
Phone:	632-1000
Days/Hours:	Brunch: Sat-Sun 9:30-2:30
	Dinner: Sun-Thurs 5-10, Fri-Sat 5-11
Reservations:	Not accepted

Simpatico is a casual trattoria that is a perfect place for families and friends to pass the evening or conclude an afternoon of browsing in the wonderful shops upstairs in Wallingford Center. Service is cheerful and the pace is relaxed. In nice weather, the outdoor brick courtyard accomodates up to 100 people under colorful umbrellas, with the Wallingford street scene screened off by abundant northwest foliage.

Nightly dinners are dominated by southern Italian-inspired items like Rigatoni Simpatico (mussels, calamari and chicken sauteed with garlic, peperoncini and Kalamata olives), and Spaghetti con Salsiccia (sausage, sweet peppers, garlic, and onions in a rich meat sauce). Simpatico's salads, especially their Granoturco Crespo made with cornmeal crepes, sweet peppers, leeks, prosciutto, and baked with several light cheeses, are imaginative in concept and worth trying.

Pizzas, baked pasta dishes and evening specials round out the choices. Children's specials for $4.95-$5.95 and antipasti for $3.75-$7.45 are available, too. Dinner entrees are $6.50-$13.95. American influences are present at weekend brunches (home fries, eggs benedict, and waffles) in addition to Italian-accented items like eggs poached with prociutto, spinach and cream. Brunch prices are $4.50-$8.95.

100 Seats + 100 Outdoors • **Full bar** • **Easy wheelchair access from street** • **Free on-street and lot parking** • **Waiting area** • **Smoking in designated area Children welcome** • *Credit cards:* **VISA M/C AmEx Local checks**

SOSTANZA

Location:	1927 43rd Ave. E., Seattle
Phone:	324-9701
Days/Hours:	Sun, Tues-Thurs 5:30-9:30,
	Fri-Sat 5:30-10
Reservations:	Accepted

Like many of the better Italian ristorantes in Seattle, Sostanza is not a stereotype. The interior is a rustic contrast of warm yellow walls with sconces casting soft light on dark wood, an open fireplace and brick floors covered with a big Oriental rug. It's both a casual neighborhood ristorante and a tasteful, well-appointed bistro. The prices and decor suggest the latter (our simple supper of two glasses of wine, Caesar salad and a plate of pasta was $30), but most of the clientele were wearing shorts and sandals. There are no hours or menus posted outside, and it can be hard to catch someone there to make a reservation.

Owner/chef Erin Rosella's menu is a fine sampler of foods and flavors of northern Italy and the Provence. Antipasti are $7.50-$9.50; salads $4.25-$6.50. *Primi* courses are $10.95-$14.50 and offer exceptional pasta dishes like tagliatelle with prawns, cannellini beans, mushrooms and basil ($14.50). Main entree courses are $14.50-$22, and include superb offerings like rabbit stuffed with prosciutto and spinach, and wood oven-roasted Guinea hen with tomato, ragout and couscous). Daily specials are, of course, available.

The wine list features primarily Tuscan, Piedmont and Veneto reds and whites, with some domestic bottles available. Prices are $14-$45. Rosella always serves excellent desserts that she makes herself.

55 Seats • Wine and beer • Wheelchair access
Free and metered on-street parking • Small waiting
area • Smoking permitted; no pipe or cigars
Credit cards: **VISA M/C AmEx Local checks**

STELLA'S

Location:	4500 - 9th Avenue NE, Seattle
Phone:	633-1100
Days/Hours:	Open 24 hours, 7 days
	Breakfast: Daily 5 am-11 am,
	Sat-Sun-Holidays 5-3
	Lunch: 11-4
	Dinner: 4-11
	Late night: 11 pm-4 am; includes breakfast
Reservations:	Suggested for dinner hours

Stella's claims to be the "best 24-hour Italian joint in town." Located in the U-District adjacent to the Metro Cinema complex, it draws late night denizens of the area, as well as cosmopolites who simply must have a plate of pasta at 2 a.m. The patrons (mild to wild) are the wonderful eclectic mix of people who make the U-District so interesting.

The four Mitchelli Trattorias (Stella's, Mitchelli, Bella Luna, Angelina's) share the same menu and wine list, with on-site chefs preparing daily specials that accomodate the differing culinary preferences of the neighborhood clientele. At Stella's you can expect a decent Italian meal, good wine and a general feeling of fun. Service is friendly and as fast as you want it to be. The menu array includes antipasti ($4.75-$6.50), soups and salads ($5-$6), pastas $5.95-$9.85), and entrees of chicken and veal for $9-$12.

The Late Nite menu is available from 11 p.m. to 4 a.m. and includes eggs, omelettes and waffles for $2.85-$5.95, and selections of antipasti, salads and soups, sandwiches and plenty of pastas.

113 Seats • Full bar • Tight wheelchair access
Free on-street parking and in lot across the street
Small waiting area • Smoking in designated area
Credit cards: **VISA M/C Local checks**

STRESA

Location:	2220 Carillon Point, Kirkland
Phone:	889-9006
Days/Hours:	Lunch: 11-4 Daily
	Dinner: 5-11 Daily
Reservations:	Recommended for weekend dinner

Should you be cruising Lake Washington and have a yen for *capellini al pomodoro e basilico* (fresh angel hair pasta with tomatoes and basil), head for the marina at Carillon Point. While you indulge yourself at Stresa, the slip is free for two hours. (Landlubbers also park free for two hours in adjacent lots.) Named for the town of Stresa that sits on the shores of Lago Maggiore north of Milan, this three-year-old restaurant offers lakeside hospitality in an exquisite setting. Wrap-around windows front a westerly view of Lake Washington; and whether dappled with sunshine or rain, the view is terrific.

Eating here can, however, take a wedge from your pocketbook. The dinner menu includes antipasti ($5-$9.50), zuppe ($4-$9.50), meat entrees with fish, chicken, veal and beef ($13.50-$19.75) and wood-fired oven pizzas ($5-$9.75). If you order a pasta entree ($9.50-$15), expect that the pasta will be made to order and that all ingredients are as fresh and authentic as possible. The *linguine "tuttomare"* (with clams, mussels and squid in light tomato sauce) is to die for, and so is the *lombata di vitello* (veal with fresh rosemary and roasted potatoes). Their own desserts, especially the gelato ($4), are memorable: the real thing. The lunch menu is an abbreviated version of dinner.

The wine cellar, too, is first-rate and priced at $15-$200. Dominated by Italian wines, you're sure to find one that suits your meal — and your pocketbook

100 Seats + 100 outdoors • **Full bar** • **Wheelchair access** • **Validated parking and boat mooring**
Waiting area • **Smoking in designated areas**
Credit cards: VISA M/C AmEx Disc Local checks

STROMBOLI'S

Location:	4135 Providence Pointe Dr., Issaquah
Phone:	392-0214
Days/Hours:	Lunch: 11:30-2 Tues-Fri
	Dinner: 5-9:30 Tues-Sun
	Brunch: Sun 11-2
Reservations:	Recommended on weekends

Stromboli's is set in the retirement community of Providence Pointe. Nearly all the restaurants in this guidebook are in neighborhoods or shopping areas, so in this regard alone it is distinctive. A security guard at the gate of Providence Pointe's entrance will direct you to Stromboli's, which is in the Town Hall building.

The environs are serene and verdant. Floor-to-ceiling windows covered with green and white striped awnings surround the restaurant, bringing in the view of tall evergreens and the foothills of Issaquah. Doors open to an aggregate patio/deck, which seats diners in warm weather who want to feel even closer to the glades and vistas. It's a lovely spot for an intimate dinner with family or a favorite companion.

The dinner menu is Italian-inspired, while the lunch menu is not. Dinner entrées include seafood fettucine, fettucine Alfredo, cannelloni, veal and seasonal seafoods. Entrees are $10.95-$16.95 and include soup or salad, fresh vegetables and bread. Specials of the house are marinated and grilled, double-thick Ellensburg lamb chops and a wonderful Veal Ossobuco. Domestic wines dominate the list. Bottles are $11-$31, and wines by the glass are $3.50-$5.

**75 Seats • Beer and wine • Wheelchair access
Free parking • Comfortable waiting area • No
smoking • *Credit cards:* VISA M/C AmEx DISC
Local checks   Entertainment '92 cards**

TESTA ROSSA

Location:	210 Broadway (upstairs), Seattle
Phone:	328-0878
Days/Hours:	Lunch and dinner feature the same menu
	Sun-Thurs 11-11, Fri-Sat 11-12
Reservations:	Accepted for parties of 5 or more

Sleek white walls hung with mixed media and oils from a local art gallery (priced to sell) and glazed terra cotta tiled floors surround diners at Testa Rossa. This casual bistro is known throughout the city for its stuffed pizzas, reputed to be the best around; but I found other fine things deserve mention, too.

Take, for example, the grilled panini ($4.95) with fillings like roasted sweet red peppers and artichokes, and the assortment of pasta salads and fresh mixed green salads ($5.50-$7.50), or the array of antipasti and homemade soups ($2.95-$7.95), or the wines by the glass at $3.50 — a Montepulciano and a Trebbiano, each an excellent example of wines from the Abruzzi region of Italy. Pasta and main entrées are $8.50-$10.95. Testa Rossa is the only Italian-style restaurant I've found that marks "heart healthy" menu items with a small heart.

It's true the pizzas are marvelous, but it's your creative genius that assembles them. You have the option of designing one with a thin crust or a stuffed (pie-like with high sides) version from assorted ingredients like sun-dried tomatoes, Kalamata olives or roasted garlic. A stuffed regular pizza that serves 2-3 people is around $16.25; a thin crust version that serves 2-3 is $15.95. Mini versions are available also, and they start at $2.50-$3.50.

100 Seats • Beer and wine • Wheelchair access thru parking garage below and up elevator • Free parking in garage below and in lot behind building • Small waiting area • No smoking • *Credit cards:* VISA M/C AmEx Local checks

TOSCANA

Location:	1312 NE 43rd St., Seattle
Phone:	547-7679
Days/Hours:	Lunch: Mon-Fri 11:30-2:30
	Dinner: Wed-Mon 5-11
Reservations:	Advised for dinner

Loosely translated, Toscana means "of Tuscany", which is owner/chef Angelo Lupianez's birthplace. Expect northern Italian fare, with delicate interpretation. The wall murals in the "lunch side" of Toscana (enter from 43rd Street) are downright Etruscan in feel and look. Angelo makes his own pasta, and he claims to have the best gnocchi in the city. (Where have we heard that before? The Great Gnocchi challenge is on!)

Meet a friend here for an excellent glass of Italian red wine ($3-$4) and a plate of Angelo's own Tortellini Buon Gusto ($6.95). Antipasti for $4.95, several salads for $4.95, and an assortment of pasta and meat dishes are available for $5.95-$6.95 either to eat on premises or to take out. All entrées include either soup or salad.

For dinner, enter from the alley on the west side of the building, which is marked by planters filled with colorful flowers. The dining room has the air of a friendly inn; overflow crowds are seated in the luncheon room. The dinner menu features decidedly Italian antipasti like stuffed artichokes and an antipasto caldo made with assorted seafoods for around $4.95, neither of which are found very often in Seattle. Main entrées of pasta, chicken and meats are offered for a reasonable $7.95-$8.95. Salads and soup are á la carte for $3.95-$4.95.

Angelo's wine list is very good, and he knows each and every bottle. Bottles are $16-$26, with some slightly higher.

90 Seats • Full bar • Wheelchair access • Metered on-street parking and lots • No waiting area Smoking in designated area

TOSONI'S

Location:	14320 NE 20th, Bellevue
Phone:	644-1668
Days/Hours:	Tues-Sat 5-10
Reservations:	Advised on weekends

It is amazing that for over nine years, Austrian-born and trained chef Walter Walcher has been cooking such imaginative, continental dinners with so little fanfare. On the other hand, if Tosoni's enlarged the small dining room and entered into the big restaurant category, chef Walter might have to forego his winter skiing and summer sailing, which is why he settled here in the first place.

On the warm summer evening I stopped in for prawns, prosciutto and melon ($10), Walter was cooking in the open kitchen wearing Dutch clogs and sporting a feather in his chef's white hat. According to the thoroughly French waiter, Tosoni's does not want "the responsibility of a set menu," I was presented with that day's offerings, which included Veal Chanterelles ($16.75), Fettuccini di Gardino ($9.50) and Halibut Duglere ($14). The menu is certainly continental, but Tosoni's reputation is for Italian food. I suggest you will have the pleasure of choosing from entrees prepared with any number of seasonal foods and unusual delights ranging from smoked duck to venison to veal and fish. Desserts, too, are exceptional. Chef Walter's sorbet made with either fresh raspberries, kiwi or fresh blackberries is wonderful.

The wine list is a mix of Italian, California and French wines for $13-$30, and house wines are $3.75 a glass.

44 Seats • Wine and Beer • Wheelchair access
Free parking in adjacent lot • No waiting area
No smoking • *Credit cards:* VISA M/C

THE TRATTORIA

Location:	9 Lake Street, Kirkland
Phone:	822-6060
Days/Hours:	Dinner: Mon 4:30-9, Tues-Thurs 4:30-10, Fri 4:30-11, Sat 4:00-11, Sun 4:30-9
	Brunch: Sun 9-3
Reservations:	Accepted

Oh, the little Italian treasures that Kirkland has to offer! It's possible to park for free, amble along among the interesting store fronts, pause at one fine little Italian restaurant for an antipasti and a glass of Valpolicella, at another for a plate of pasta and a glass of Chianti Classico, and finish off the excurion at yet another with coffee and zabaglione. In your wanderings, stop in at The Trattoria for excellent service, a view of Lake Washington, an Italian tenor on tape and a stylish interior.

The Trattoria has a a very good antipasto bar, as well as an array of antipasti from which to choose. We ordered the antipasto misto, a generous assortment of selections from the antipasto bar for $6.25. It was superb and was plenty for two. Pastas come with a choice of soup or salad. The Spaghetti Puttanesca is robust, full of heat, garlic, and tomato; the Fettucine Gamberetti con Pesto (prawns sauteed with fresh basil and garlic) was unexpectedly rich but very good. Specials of the house with chicken, veal, and fish round out the menu. Prices are $6.75-$10.95 and include soup or salad, pasta, and vegetables.

Sunday breakfast bows to purely American preferences for Belgian waffles, bacon and eggs, hot cakes and Denver omelettes. Prices are a reasonable $4.50-$7.95.

**75 Seats • Full bar • Tight wheelchair access
Free on-street parking • Bar/waiting area
Smoking in designated area • *Credit cards:* VISA
M/C AmEx Local checks**

TRATTORIA MITCHELLI

Location:	84 Yesler Way, Seattle
Phone:	623-3883
Days/Hours:	Breakfast: Mon-Fri 7-11
	Brunch: Sat-Sun 8 am-2pm
	Lunch: Daily 11-4
	Dinner: Daily 4-11
	Late Night: 11 pm-4 am
Reservations:	Recommended for dinner hours

"The Trat" has been in Pioneer Square 14 years, and except for its new pizza bar, it has changed very little over time. Seattle isn't known as a late-night city, but at 3 a.m. you'll find crowds here from the opera, theater and symphony along with numerous insomniac artists gathered over Caffe Mauro and eggs discussing the latest in the arts scene. During the day, you sit on the same worn leather seats and watch groups of tourists descending into the Seattle Underground across the street.

The "fused" northern and southern Italian dishes feature rich cream sauces, various polentas, legumes, hearty meat sauces, and fresh salads. There are always "blackboard specials." Lunch prices are $4.95-$8.25, and dinners are $5.35-$12.50. Breakfasts include omelettes, eggs and waffles and are $2-$6. Plenty of coffee and espresso drinks are available.

Trattoria Mitchelli has a good wine list, but serious enophiles should ask for their reserve wine list. From local purveyors and occasional trips to Italy, owner Danny Mitchell has assembled a cellar of world-class Barolos, Barbarescos, Chiantis and other classic Italian wines that sell for up to $275 a bottle.

110 Seats + 90 in bar • Full bar • Easy wheelchair access • Metered on-street parking and numerous private lots • Small waiting area • Kids welcome Smoking in designated areas • *Credit Cards:* VISA M/C AmEx Discover Local checks

UMBERTO'S

Location:	100 South King Street, Seattle
Phone:	621-0575
Days/Hours:	Lunch: Mon-Fri 11-5, limited service in bar only 2:30-5
	Dinner: Mon-Thurs 5-10, Fri-Sat 5-11, Sun 4:30-9
Reservations:	Recommended

Most of this 10-year-old restaurant in Pioneer Square is below street level. Carefully placed track lighting spots a central service bar, plants and banners. The terra cotta tile floor and exposed brick walls contrast with splashes of neon here and there. Underlying this patina of a casual uptown restaurant is a consistent attention to quality and good food that has long attracted a professional, stylish clientele.

Head chef David Stetter changes the menu to accomodate seasonal foods. Thankfully, however, he keeps some of his standouts. Try the radiatore pepperoncini, the fettuccini grigliata, or the cappelini d'angelo. For a luncheon salad eater, I recommend Umberto's al fresco plate or classic Caesar. Lunch entrees come in small or regular portion sizes. Complementing the meals are Grand Central's Como Bread and Torrefazione coffee. Dinner entree prices range from $7.99-$15.99. Lunches are $6.99-$9.99; small portions are slightly lower in price.

If you stop in for a meal prior to a Seahawks or Mariner's game, be sure to let the host know where you're headed. Umberto's has pre-game fast service and brunches before afternoon Seahawks games.

150+ Seats • Full bar • Wheelchair access
Parking in paid lots or metered on-street • Small
waiting area • Smoking in designated area; no pipes
or cigars, please. • *Credit cards:* **VISA M/C**
Discover AmEx Local checks Entertainment '92 cards

VERRAZANO'S

Location:	28835 Pacific Highway So., Federal Way
Phone:	946-4122
Days/Hours:	Lunch: Mon-Fri 11:30-4
	Dinner: Mon-Thurs 4-9, Fri-Sun 4-10
	Lounge hours: call for specifics.
	Outdoor decks open May 1
Reservations:	Recommended for dinner hours

Verrazano's has become something of an institution for people in the Federal Way-Des Moines area. Naming their restaurant for the Verrazano-Narrows Bridge that spans New York Harbor, native New Yorkers Ron Nacinovich and Pete Fischer capture the essence of American-style Italian food, and they give it to us here in abundance — as well as a sweeping view of the Olympics and Puget Sound, good service, volleyball (!), and two heated outdoor decks with full dinner and bar service when it's even half-way warm. They also have a "Lighter Fare" menu for those of us who must count calories.

The lunch and dinner menus are expansive, if not a bit overwhelming. Pasta, seafood, pizza, baked dishes, house specialties, steaks, veal, chicken, and on and on. We sampled the Seafood Verrazano's, a delicious mix of clams, prawns, scallops, mussels, and salmon sauteed in a light garlic-wine sauce. The dessert cart also proved to be abundant, so I opted for a cup of Terrafazione coffee. Dinner entrées range from $8.95-$19.95 and include soup or salad. Lunch prices are $2.75 for a bowl of soup to $9.95 for a seafood salad.

A word to the wise — don't just drop by without a reservation — this is a very popular place.

120 Seats + outdoors in season • **Full bar** • **Easy wheelchair access** • **Free parking** • **Waiting area Smoking in designated area** • *Credit cards:* **VISA M/C AmEx Discover Diner's Club Local checks**

VINCE'S

Locations:	15223 4th SW, Burien, 246-8180
	32411 Pacific Hwy S., Federal Way,
	839-1496 or 927-7727
	8824 Renton Ave. S., 722-2116
	605 Queen Anne Ave S., 283-9353
	6218 6th Ave., Tacoma, 564-7994
Days/Hours	Lunch: Mon-Sun 11-4
	Dinner: Mon-Sat 5-1, Sun 5-12
Reservations:	Required for 10+ people, recommended
	for weekends

Vince's is a near-perfect example of the Americanization of a southern Italian bistro. Owner Enzo "Vince" Mottola hit on a formula in 1957, and it continues to thrive. There are little fat candles in plastic mesh on each table, the lighting is reddish-yellow, the seats are covered with red vinyl, there's fake brick on the walls, and the ever-present tenor is singing Italian opera on tape.

Pizzas, sandwiches, pasta, and main entrees of meat, fish, and poultry are served in ample portions. My companions and I had tortellini alla paesana, calzone and penne with meat sauce. All were good, sturdy dishes designed to assure you that you are eating something Italian. Families are a big percentage of the clientele because of the reasonable prices and the predictability of the food. There's plenty of red sauce and mozzarella cheese, meatballs and spaghetti. You'll be full when you leave, the tab won't shock you, and I guarantee you'll go back because of the near-camp atmosphere.

Main entree prices range from $5.50-$12 and include soup, salad and bread. Lunches are slightly less.

226 Seats • Full bar • Easy wheelchair access
Free parking • Waiting area • Children welcome
Designated smoking area (no pipes or cigars)
Credit cards: **VISA M/C Discover Local checks**

ITALIAN WINES

Italy grows more grapes and produces more wine than any country on earth—especially red wines. In fact, wine authority Hugh Johnson describes Rome "...as a capital city with wine so much in its veins that such artificial obstructions as bottles and corks have traditionally been foreign to it." In Italy, no meal is complete without wine; and except for selling significant tonnage of their grapes to France for blending with French wines, historically Italians have consumed most of their wines themselves. But just as communication and transportation have eroded the internal barriers in Italy, so have they caused Italy's superb wines to be discovered by a global market increasingly thirsty for quality wines.

The challenge, however, is to develop a working familiarity with the vast array of available choices. As styles of food vary from region to region in Italy, so do the wines. There are more than 4,000 different wines, each with a multi-syllable name, an indistinguishable place of origin, and a mysterious grape variety shown on the label. "What am I getting, anyway?" you ask yourself as you study a bewildering array of choices. "And what does all this stuff on the label mean?"

Because I'm not an Italian enophile, I've sought assistance from the experts. I've sampled, taken notes and learned enough to offer you some helpful guidelines. Described here are the principal red and white wines from the major wine-producing regions of Italy which you will likely encounter on a wine list. The "brand," that is, the producer of the wine you're considering, and the quality vary year to year. In my wanderings among Italian restaurants, I have discovered that many offer exceptional selections and educated staff to assist you, if you ask for help.

One final note. If you are not too adventuresome and are picky about such things, play it safe and order a wine that has the "DOC" or "DOCG" stamp or label on the bottle. This stands for *denominazione di origine controlla*, which is a uniform performance standard established by producers in a specific region for wines vinified in that region. (That's "quality control" in American lingo.) The "G" in the DOCG stamped wines stands for "*garantita*." The inference is that these are "officially guaranteed" to be Italy's best wines.

If you come across a "*riserva*," know that it has been aged a prescribed number of years according to DOC standards. A "*classico*" is a wine from the classic center of a DOC zone (usually the best area) so it should exemplify the primary characteristics of that wine. Wines not covered by a DOC are classified as "*vino da tavola*" (table wine), which is the basic European category for blended wines. There are many splendid wines made in nontraditional ways that bear this designation.

RED WINES

Region: PIEDMONT
Wine Variety: BARBARESCO

A robust red wine of great character, with an intense, yet delicate, fruity bouquet and a dry, velvety finish. A perfect companion to strong cheeses, roasted meats and game dishes. One of Italy's DOCG wines, it can be heavy with tannins even when mature. Aged a minimum of two years, four years for *riserva*. Vinified from the splendid Nebbiolo grape.

Wine Variety: BARBERA

There are a number of Barberas grown in the Piedmont. A full-bodied ruby red wine with a fruity fragrance and a lively pleasant taste. A good one can be astringent and full of plum flavor. Excellent with soups, risotto, broiled meats, cheese.

Wine Variety: BAROLO

Known as the "king of wines and wine of kings," Barolos are powerful, full-bodied, and not for the faint-of-heart wine drinker. They are the most majestic expression of the Nebbiolo grape Italy offers. Barolos will often carry tannins, a deep purple color and a bouquet of violets, incense, plums, berries or truffles. Most wine experts agree that Barolos are at their best after aging 10 years, but five years earns a *riserva* designation. Barolos bear the DOCG stamp. Try a Barolo with hearty entrees such as game and roasted meats, and let the bottle breathe before you sample it.

Wine Variety: DOLCETTO

A refreshing red wine with a deep violet hue and wonderful fruity bouquet. Depending on who vinifies the grape, a Dolcetto can grip your tongue with concentrated flavor and a very dry finish, or it can be brisk, lively and soft at the finish. Ask your server, as there is definite variety among the Dolcetto styles. All should bear the DOC stamp and they are best drunk young. A superb accompaniment to vegetable dishes and simple meats.

Wine Variety: NEBBIOLO

I have yet to taste a Nebbiolo that is a disappointment. It is a sturdy, full-bodied red wine with lots of fruit (usually plums or raspberries) and a velvety finish. Nebbiolos may be DOCS or *vino da tavola*; if you order one that is 4-6 years old, you will experience the full expression of this grape. Nebbiolo grapes are the base for Barolo, Barbesco, and Gattinara wines, too. Enjoy with hearty pastas, roasted meats such as beef or pork, and aged cheeses.

Region: TUSCANY
Wine Variety: BRUNELLO di MONTALCINO

Aged a long time (usually 3-5 years in the barrel and then several years in the bottle), this is a concentrated, powerful red wine. It is rich, complex, with a heady bouquet and a dry finish with essence of plums and intense fruit. It is a superb complement to red meats, hearty pasta and other toothsome foods. Often cited as a premium Italian wine bearing the DOCG designation.

Wine Variety: CHIANTI

The quintessential wine associated with Italy, Chianti can be vinified for drinking young, or it can age and develop into a wonderfully fruity, robust, dry, refined wine. It can bear spicy floral bouquets, delicate with blackberries or almonds, even hints of vanilla; expect a lot of fruit and color. Aged three years, it gets a *riserva* rating. Always order a *classico* and you won't be disappointed. It is an excellent complement to grilled red meats, veal, tomato-based pasta dishes, duck or lamb. (Or just drink it by itself! A good *classico* can make crackers and cheeze-from-a-can a holiday.)

Wine Variety: MONTEPULCIANO

A full-bodied, fruity, dry red wine, rich with life and warmth, excellent with hearty pastas, grilled meats and vegetables, and anything you would eat with a Chianti Classico or a Brunello. The Montepulciano grape is grown in several regions of Italy. Abruzzi in the south produces more than a million cases annually. The Vino Nobile di Montepulciano from Tuscany is a DOCG wine.

Region: VENETO
Wine Variety: BARDOLINO

Bardolino is a lighter version of Valpolicella, also good consumed young. It is cherry red, lively, fresh and fruity, with a delicate bouquet and pleasant dry finish. It is very good slightly chilled with pastas, ham, veal and poultry.

Wine Variety: VALPOLICELLA

A wine with a wide range of qualities, it is usually deep ruby red in color, full of fruit, but rather light and dry. It is good drunk young, especially the year after its vintage. Choose ones that are designated as *classico*. Enjoy Valpolicella with beef, hearty pasta and poultry.

Footnote: *Merlot, Cabernet Franc and Cabernet Sauvignon are major red wine grapes brought into Italy from France hundreds of years ago. They are widely used in blended wines and are also frequently found as table wines. Since they are not indigenous grapes, they will not carry the DOC stamp, but rather vino da tavola designation.*

WHITE WINES

Region: LATIUM
Wine Variety: FRASCATI

A golden white wine that can be either dry or sweet, depending on the vintner. The dry wines are full-flavored, nutty and soft on the finish. Drink young and enjoy it as an aperitif or with light pastas, chicken, smoked meats and flavorful creamy cheeses. Order DOC Frascatis, since *vini da tavolas* reputedly do not travel well.

Region: THE MARCHES
Wine Variety: VERDICCHIO

A dry white wine that is a commercial success. Over one million cases a year are produced. You will often see it on wine lists. Usually fruity, clean, refreshing and excellent with all seafood, pesto pasta dishes and poultry. Drink it young.

Region: PIEDMONT
Wine Variety: GAVI

Made from the Cortese grape, Gavi is fresh, young, with a mild acidity and rich floral bouquet and fruity flavor. It is a fine companion with light antipasti, fish, risotto or vegetable pasta dishes.

Region: UMBRIA
Wine Variety: ORVIETO

One of the better known popular Italian white wines, the adjective "mild" seems to override everything: a mild fruity bouquet, medium body, pale in color and slightly sweet in finish. Chilled, it is a good sipping wine for the afternoon, or to have with fruits and mild cheeses. Order a DOC *classico*.

Region: VENETO
Wine Variety: PINOT GRIGIO

Pinot Grigio is also grown in Emilia-Romagna, Trentino-Alto Adige and Friuli-Venezie Giulia. Those origins will be shown on the label. It is characterized by a clean, crisp and delicately balanced taste, sometimes with a hint of lemon or a grassy cast to the flavor. A lovely aromatic wine to enjoy with pasta dishes, cold soups, salads and seafood, or by itself as a sipping wine.

Wine Variety: SOAVE

Soave is the most popular of all Italian white wines. It is smooth, light, fresh, easy to drink, with lots of fruit and a distinct spicy bouquet. It is delicious with pastas, salads, most seafood, poultry and light meat dishes, or slightly chilled with cheeses and fruits.

Footnote: *Chardonnay and Sauvignon Blanc are French grapes imported from France and widely grown in major wine producing regions of Italy. They are used in blended wines, but you will also find them on many wine lists under their own name. Because they are not indigenous to Italy, Chardonnays and Sauvignon Blancs will not carry the DOC stamp, but rather vino da tavola designation.*

GLOSSARY OF COMMONLY-FOUND ITALIAN MENU ITEMS AND TERMS

Often we dine at Italian ristorantes where the menu items do not include a description of the dish, and we must rely on a server's description of the food or our own inhibited responses. It's not so complicated as it all sounds—mainly because most places in Seattle serve many of the same things. A careful reading of menus gathered during my research showed the following frequently appearing terms and entrees. I trust the definitions and/or explanations of them will be helpful to you.

Please remember that these are basic, general descriptions. Good chefs will add their own "signature" ingredients to the recipe, which is one of the great joys of Italian cooking.

Acciughe - Anchovies

Aglio Olio - aglio is garlic; olio is olive oil. Generally the oil is infused with garlic and tossed with pasta.

Agnello - Lamb

Alfredo - A rich white sauce made with cream, butter and (generally) fresh basil and garlic and served on fettuccine pasta. Herbs are the signature of the cook.

alla Diavola - Meat rubbed with black pepper ("hot as the devil"), marinated in oil and lemon, then grilled. Southern style often substitutes red pepper flakes to create the "heat."

Arrosto - Pan roasted, as in *vitello arrosto*

Bistecca - Beefsteak

Bolognese sauce - A sauce of white wine, milk, tomatoes, various vegetables and beef (any number of varieties may be used from sausage to lean stew beef) and served with chef's choice of pasta.

Bruschetta - crusty Italian bread brushed with olive oil and garlic and roasted or broiled. Often cooks will top the brushchetta with any combination of garnish: Kalamata olives, fresh tomato slices, fresh basil, capers, etc.

Burro - Butter

Calamari - Squid (can be fried, stewed, sauteed)

Cannelloni - Meat stuffed pasta (usually beef or unsmoked ham called prosciutto), seasoned with a tomato/meat sauce and a thin bechamel (white) sauce. Often topped with melted cheese.
Herbs and other flavorings are cook's choice.

Capers - Buds of a small bush that have been cured in brine or salt. They are a dusty green in color and add a pungent, smokey tartness to food.

Carbonara - A white sauce of cream, eggs, garlic, pancetta (Italian bacon) and usually Parmesan or asiago cheese. Herbs, seasonings are whim of the cook. Sauce is served with pasta.

Carne - A collective term for meat

Carpaccio - Rare roast beef sliced paper thin and served with lemon, olive oil, artichokes, cheese—or whatever chef designs.

Carciofi - Artichokes; an extremely popular Italian vegetable.

Cioppino - A fish/seafood stew

Cozze - Fresh mussels

della Casa - "Of the house", a house special

del Giorno - "of the day", as in "soup of the day"

Dolci - Literally "sweet", but is used as a descriptive term for dessert.

Fagioli - A collective term for dry beans

Florentine - "In Florence; in the Florentine way." Often used to describe entrees that include spinach.

Fritta - Fried

Frittata - Open-faced Italian omelet

Frutti di mare - A variety of fish, shellfish (literally "fruits of the sea").

Focaccia - A flat, thin, crusty bread often infused with any of the following ingredients: coarse pepper or salt, garlic or onion bits, fresh herbs. In the U.S it may be topped with ingredients and baked or broiled.

Funghi - Mushrooms; *funghi secchi* are dried (wild) mushrooms

Gamberetti - Shrimp

Gnocchi - A small, dumpling-shaped pasta made with pureed potato or semolina flour, filled with ground herbs, vegetables or meat, and boiled. Gnocchi may be served with a marinara, cream, or pesto sauce.

Gorgonzola - A mild, flavorful Italian bleu cheese

Insalate - Salad

Kalamata Olives - Salty Greek olives that are cured in brine and vinegar.

Marinara - A red sauce made with fresh tomatoes, fresh herbs and seasonings. The latter ingredients are the choice of the cook and might include sweet basil, rosemary, parsley, oregano, garlic and onions. Marinara sauce may be served with pasta, seafood and some meat dishes.

Milanese - After the fashion of Milan

Misto - Literally means "mixed" and is used to describe mixed meats, mixed greens, mixed seafood (misti is plural).

Ossobuco - Braised veal shanks simmered in broth with herbs and vegetables—each of which is cook's choice.

Pancetta - Italian bacon, almost always unsmoked.

Pane - Bread

Panini - Croutons

Peperoncino - Sweet red or green peppers

Peperoncino rosso - Hot red peppers

Pesce - A collective term for fish

Pesto - A green (verde) sauce of fresh basil, garlic, olive oil, and other fresh herbs of the cook's choosing that are ground to a puree and served with pasta, gnocchi, seafoods or meats.

Piselli - Green sweet peas

Polenta - Popular in northern Italian regions, polenta is a dense, robust predecessor to American cornbread. Cornmeal is cooked with water, then allowed to set up so it can be sliced into squares. Onions, peperoncini or other ingredients may be added. After the polenta sets, it may be grilled with fresh vegetables or topped with a marinara sauce and sausage, or served alone broiled hot with cheese.

Pollo - Chicken

Primavera - Made with fresh vegetables

Prosciutto - Italian ham that is usually unsmoked, thinly sliced, heavily marbled.

Puttanesca - A highly flavored tomato-base sauce made with capers, black olives, peperoncino rosso (hot red peppers), anchovies—or whatever the chef chooses. Puttanesca is served with pasta.

Quatro Frommagi - Literally "four cheeses." Usually will include a combination of mozzarella, gorgonzola, Parmesan, Romano, ricotta, fontina, or asiago cheeses.

Risotto - Rice that has been sauteed with butter and onions, then simmered in a flavored stock. Vegetables, herbs, cheese or shellfish may be added. Risotto is often served as a first course (*primi*) in Italian meals, just as pasta and gnocchi might be.

Saltimbocca - Veal cooked in a butter and wine sauce with prosciutto, mushrooms, seasonings, herbs and sometimes a mild cheese. Variations are the whim of the cook.

Salsiccia - A term used to describe dishes that feature chopped or ground meats like sausage.

Scaloppine - Small thinly sliced or pounded medallions of meat; the most celebrated is the sweet, lean scaloppine di vitello that is sauteed and served with a delicate sauce such as lemon or Marsala.

Vitello - Veal

Vitello Parmigiana - Veal lightly breaded, seasoned with Parmesan cheese and topped with marinara sauce.

Vitello Piccata - Veal served with a sauce of lemon, butter and capers.

ALPHABETICAL LISTING

GAMBARDELLA'S PASTA BELLA, 1313 West Meeker, Kent, 30

GASPARE'S, 8051 Lake City Way NE, Seattle, 31

GENE'S, 212 S.3rd, Kent, 32

GIANCARLO, 4624 SW 320th, Federal Way, 33

GIUSEPPE'S, 144-105th NE, Bellevue, 34

GRAZIE CAFFEE ITALIANO, Bellevue, Tacoma, Tukwila, 35

IL BISTRO, 93-A Pike Street, Seattle, 36

IL PAESANO, 5628 University Way NE, Seattle, 37

IL TERRAZZO CARMINE, 411 1st Ave.S., Seattle, 38

ITALIA, 1010 Western Ave., Seattle, 39

ITALIAN GARDENS, 1309 Auburn Way, Auburn, 40

JAY-BERRY'S, 385 NW Gilman Blvd, Issaquah, 41

LA DOLCE VITA, 3428 NE 55th, Seattle, 42

LOFURNO'S, 2060 15th W., Seattle, 43

LOMBARDI'S CUCINA, Ballard and Issaquah, 44

MAMMA MELINA'S, 4759 Roosevelt Way, Seattle, 45

MIA ROMA, 7614 Bothell Way, Kenmore, 46

PALOMINO, 3rd Floor, Pacific First Centre, 5th & Pike, Seattle, 47

PAPA LUIGI'S, 31406 Pacific Hwy S., Federal Way, 48

PASTA BELLA, Ballard and Seattle (Queen Anne), 49

PINK DOOR, 1919 Post Alley, Seattle, 50

PIZZUTO'S, 5032 Wilson, Seattle, 51

POGACHA, 119-106th Ave NE, Bellevue, 52

POOR ITALIAN CAFE, 2000 Second Ave. at Virginia, Seattle, 53

PORTOBELLO, 30333 Pacific Highway S., Federal Way, 54

RISTORANTE MACHIAVELLI, 1215 Pine, Seattle, 55

RISTORANTE PARADISO, 120 Park Lane, Kirkland, 56

RISTORANTE PONY, 621-1/2 Queen Anne Ave., Seattle, 57

RISTORANTE di RAGAZZI, 2329 California Ave SW, West Seattle, 58

SALEH AL LAGO, 6804 Green Lake Way, Seattle, 59

SALUTE, 3410 NE 55th, Seattle, 60

SALUTE IN CITTA, 620 Stewart (Vance Hotel), Seattle, 61

SALVATORE, 6100 Roosevelt Way NE, Seattle, 62

SERAFINA, 2043 Eastlake Ave, Seattle, 63

SIMPATICO, 4430 Wallingford, Seattle, 64

SOSTANZA, 1927 43rd Ave E., Seattle, 65

STELLA'S, 4500-9th Ave NE, Seattle, 66

STRESA, 2220 Carillon Point, Kirkland, 67

STROMBOLI'S, 4135 Providence Pointe Dr., Issaquah, 68

TESTAROSSA, 210 Broadway, Seattle, 69

TOSCANA, 1312 NE 43rd, Seattle, 70

TOSONI'S, 14320 NE 20th, Bellevue, 71

THE TRATTORIA, 9 Lake St., Kirkland, 72

TRATTORIA MITCHELLI, 84 Yesler Way, Seattle, 73

UMBERTO'S, 100 S. King St., Seattle, 74

VERRAZANO'S, 28835 Pacific Hwy S., Federal Way, 75

VINCE'S, Queen Anne, Rainier Beach, Burien, Renton, Federal Way and Tacoma, 76

RESTAURANTS BY NEIGHBORHOOD

KIRKLAND
Calabria Ristorante Italiano, 23
DaVinci's, 27
Cafe Juanita, 20
Ristoranti Paradiso, 56
Stresa, 67
The Trattoria, 72

LAKE CITY
Gaspare's Ristorante Italiano, 31

LAKE UNION EAST
Serafina, 63

LAKE UNION SOUTH
Cucina! Cucina!, 26

LAKEWOOD
Pizzuto's Italian Cafe, 51

MADISON PARK/MOUNTLAKE
Cafe Lago, 21
Sostanza, 65

MERCER ISLAND
Caffee Italia, 22

PIKE PLACE MARKET
Il Bistro, 36
Pink Door, 50

PIONEER SQUARE
Al Boccalino, 9
AntiPasti, 11
Botticelli Cafe e Rosticceria, 17
Celebrity Italian Kitchen
Il Terrazzo Carmine, 38
Trattoria Mitchelli, 73
Umberto's, 74

QUEEN ANNE
Buongusto, 19
Lofurno's, 43
Pasta Bella, 49
Ristorante Pony, 57
Vince's, 76

RENTON
Armondo's Cafe Italiano, 12
Gene's, 32
Vince's, 76

TUKWILA
Cucina!Cucina!, 26
Grazie Caffe Italiano, 35

UNIVERSITY DISTRICT
Avé! Al Ristorante Italiano, 13
Il Paesano Ristorante Italiano, 37
Mamma Melina's, 45
Stella's, 66
Toscana, 71

BEST ITALIAN RESTAURANTS FOR FAMILIES

While every restaurant welcomes families, some are definitely more conducive to kids because of seating, ambiance, prices and menu offerings. Here, in my opinion, are the ones that best accomodate families.

Angelina's Trattoria, 10
2311 California SW, West Seattle

Armondo's Cafe Italiano, 12
919 So. 3rd, Renton

Ave'! Ristorante Italiano, 13
4743 University Way NE, Seattle (University District)

Barlee's Family Pizza & Pasta, 14
3410 Fremont Ave., Seattle (Fremont District)

Bella Luna, 15
14053 Greenwood Ave. N., Seattle (Greenwood District)

Calabria Ristorante Italiano, 23
132 Lake, Kirkland

DaVinci's, 27
89 Kirkland Ave., Kirkland

Filiberto's Italian Restaurant & Deli, 29
144th & Des Moines Way So., Burien

Giancarlo, 33
4624 SW 320th, Federal Way

Giuseppe's Italian Restaurant & Lounge, 34
144 105th NE, Bellevue

Jay-Berry's, 41
385 NW Gilman Blvd., Issaquah

Lombardi's Cucina, 44
2200 NW Market, Ballard
719 Gilman Blvd., Issaquah

Italian Gardens, 40
1309 Auburn Way N., Auburn

Papa Luigi's, 48
31406 Pacific Hwy So., Federal Way

Pasta Bella, 49
5909 15th Ave. NW, Ballard
1530 Queen Anne Ave. N., Seattle (Queen Anne Hill)

Pizzuto's Italian Cafe, 51
5032 Wilson, Seattle (Lakewood)

Portobello, 54
30333 Pacific Hwy So., Federal Way

Simpatico, 64
4430 Wallingford, Seattle (Wallingford Center)

The Trattoria, 72
9 Lake St., Kirkland

Trattoria Mitchelli, 73
84 Yesler Way, Seattle (Pioneer Square)

Vince's, 76
All locations

NOTES

NOTES

_____

_____

_____

_____

_____

_____

_____

_____

_____

_____

_____

_____

_____

_____

_____

_____

_____

_____

_____

Merilee Frets has 14 years of public relations, writing and marketing experience in the arts, education and food. She has extensive culinary and wine knowledge and recently edited a 200-page cookbook *Cooking with Lentils & Split Peas: The Pulse of Life*. She lives in Federal Way with her husband John Bonnier, a chef and 15-year owner of a lunch and supper house. She also has a fantastically brilliant and talented daughter, Shauna, who loves peanut butter and jelly sandwiches and makes extensive use of their microwave.

Photo of author taken at Giancarlo in Federal Way.